Amending the Abject Body

SUNY series in Feminist Criticism and Theory
Michelle A. Massé, editor

Amending the Abject Body

Aesthetic Makeovers in Medicine and Culture

DEBORAH CASLAV COVINO

Published by
State University of New York Press, Albany

For information, address State University of New York Press,
State University Plaza, Albany, NY 12246

Production, Kelli Williams
Marketing, Anne Valentine

Library of Congress Cataloging-in-Publication Data

Covino, Deborah Caslav, 1960–
    Amending the abject body: aesthetic makeovers in medicine and culture/Deborah Caslav
Covino.
        p. cm. —(SUNY series in feminist criticism and theory)
    Includes bibliographical references and index.
    ISBN 0-7914-6231-5 —ISBN 0-7914-6232-3 (pbk.)
    1. Body image in women. 2. Self-perception in women. 3. Women—Physiology. 4. Body,
Human—Social aspects. 5. Surgery, Plastic. 6. Feminist theory. I. Title. II. Series.

BF697 .5B63C67 2004
306.4'613—dc22

2004043372

TO BILL, MY HEART'S CONTENT

Contents

Acknowledgments

For their early support, I am grateful to my teachers and mentors at the University of Illinois at Chicago: Clark Hulse, Peggy McCracken, James Sosnoski, Michael Lieb, and Donald Marshall. The Department of English at Florida Atlantic University provided me the time and encouragement so essential to this project. James Peltz, Kelli Williams, and the SUNY Press staff have guided this project through with understanding, good advice, and care. I'm especially grateful to my children, Lexie and Danny, for giving up part of their mother to the demands of scholarship. Love and thanks to my mother, Brigitte Caslav, who taught me compassion, and to my father, Peter Caslav, who has the soul of a writer. Finally, thanks to Dan Cook for frequent talks about Bruce Springsteen and assorted other (less important) matters that afforded me many hours of happy distraction.

Portions of chapter 3 were adapted from "Outside-In: Body, Mind, and Self in the Advertisement of Aesthetic Surgery," which appeared in the *Journal of Popular Culture* 35.3 (Winter 2001). Portions of the introduction and chapter 1 were adapted from "Abject Criticism," which appeared in *Genders* 32 (2000).

Introduction

Feminist critics have been particularly vocal about the fortunes and misfortunes of body-image conformity. Their concerns establish many of the questions that continue to occupy us in the early twenty-first century, as the aesthetic surgical industry's prominence and influence upon prevailing conceptions and narratives of body image become increasingly widespread. In this context, it may no longer be useful or effective to continue the debate over whether this industry is or is not doing harm; rather, we might begin to inventory without complacency those practices, expectations, desires, and appeals that have become embedded in a public sense of the possible. Doing so should not, however, confuse alertness to ambiguity with ambivalence: the aesthetic surgical industry does capitalize on our desires and fears, and industry practices are often a corruption of what medicine's role in the protection and management of our bodies ought to be. For instance, while the industry claims to prize an integration of mind and body that promotes mental health, it also prizes bodies that are untroubled by agedness, physical impairment, gender ambiguity, and racial or ethnic difference. The unmodified, unimproved body is always a potential violator of the aesthetic stasis upon which happiness depends. As the industry story goes, in order for the body not to impinge upon psychological and spiritual well-being, its ailing or unacceptable parts must be cut, lasered, or refined away. This story prompts and reinforces the conception of a body that needs to be controlled, so that this industry is not so much recovering the body in our social, cultural, psychological, and aesthetic registers as it is reproving it.

The industry is certainly not the founder of oppressive aesthetic values, nor even the sole engineer of its own participation in them,[1] but it is nonetheless a part of the contemporary development of a bodily imaginary that gathers our concepts of psychological health and community around aesthetic considerations. The industry has successfully legitimated itself as a medical practice that addresses real psychological pain; it is, however, complicit in the reproduction of that pain. The cultural imaginary it informs does include the more acceptably benevolent practices of medicine as healing, yet these are also born of the exigency to avert difference, pain, mutability, and mortality, so that aesthetic healing, involved as it is in normalizing the body, defines and maintains a cultural hegemony of the normal. Further, to the extent that medicine has generally operated at the juncture of the desire to escape from the temporal and the admission of the impossibility of such escape, aesthetic surgery—which brackets away that impossibility—contributes to an emergent medical ethic that associates "good medicine" with transcendence.[2]

The aesthetic surgical industry, and the imaginary it reinforces, provide the forum for this study of the abject body in culture. The study of abjection is, especially in this context, a study of desire and its discontents. The desire that the industry invokes is one well established in psychoanalytic theory, that is, the fantasized image of oneself as free from the visible signs of temporality, discontinuity, and variance. Lacan's "Mirror Stage" presents a useful working conception of this fantasy, since it theorizes an imaginary identification with an other who is whole, from the perspective of a self who is fragmented: the imaginary here is both the object and fulfillment of desire, and is approached through the symbolic. In other words, the self that I cannot be is repeatedly symbolized in the narratives of desire that constitute my cultural identity. The confrontation between the desiring and the desired self, who I am and who I would become, implies a sort of "before-and-after" picture, analogous to those presented both visually and discursively by the aesthetic surgical industry.

Widely used in industry advertising and trade books, "before" pictures show us body parts and regions (eyes without faces; heads without torsos; isolated breasts or buttocks or thighs) described in terms that allege estrangement from youth (furrowed, lined, spotted, damaged, creased skin), from vitality (sleepy eyelids, weak chin), from proportion and symmetry (pendulous breasts, pot belly), and from whiteness (Asian eyes). "After" pictures show us these same parts after they have been removed, smoothed, slimmed, adjusted, sculpted. In both the before and after worlds, the focus remains on the area whose deviance is reparable; in such a context, the body is represented less as a dynamic of elements and processes constituting a distinctive and physically complex identity, than as a confederation of territories that can each be demarcated for upgrading or renovation. Such compartmentalization encourages us to understand our deviance from social norms and ideals as local and manageable, and to repress the full extent and range of bodily imperfection and difference.

The removal of excess and worn flesh in today's aesthetic surgical clinic corresponds with contemporary virtualizations of the body, so that the postoperative aesthetic patient is a creature of refitted parts who approximates as closely as possible the digitalized preoperative projection of her new self. These tendencies become strikingly explicit on the hundreds of web pages that feature digital photographs of patients who have undergone common procedures. Cosmeticsurgery.com, which features a national listing of aesthetic surgeons and a survey of all major procedures, opens in November 2000 with "Welcome to the Body Electric," emblematized by the bronze sculpture of an ideally proportioned woman standing in front of a giant computer keyboard. The virtualized woman is also a hypertext link: clicking on "her," we reach the page inviting the harvest of body parts. Here, the bronze woman appears again, larger, with blue boxes drawn around seven zones—head, arms, breast, abdomen, buttocks, thighs, and calves—framed by the following text:

Pick the area you would like to improve

Head (face, neck, and hair)

Arms (sagging skin, excess fat flab, etc.)

Breast (sagging, too big, too small, uneven, etc.)

Abdomen (excess fat, excess skin hanging down, etc.)

Buttocks (too fat, saggy, etc.)

Thighs (excess fat, cellulite, etc.)

Calves (too small, too fat, etc.)

Clicking on each zone produces subdivisions; for instance, the head page shows us the bronze head separated into eight zones, with this text:

Pick the area you would like to improve

Hair (for baldness, thinning hair, etc.)

Upper Eyes (tired-looking eyes, sad, small, etc.)

Lower Eyes (tired-looking eyes, bags, extra skin, etc.)

Ears (excess fat, excess skin hanging down, etc.)

Nose (too big, too small, too wide, too narrow, etc.)

Mouth (enhance the lips, improve wrinkles, etc.)

Neck (fix sagging skin, take away excess fat, etc.)

Face

    Facelift

    Skin Resurfacing (Laser)

    Skin Resurfacing (Chemical Peel)

A number of observations emerge from this example: (1) The ideal body is an aesthetic image, conceived and presented as or in a medium other than flesh; (2) The aestheticized body is achieved by identifying unwanted excess parts, and dumping them for those that more closely approximate the dead representation of the ideal outcome; (3) The aestheticized body is a universal site of desire, and thus, as Jean Baudrillard says in "Plastic Surgery for the Other," a process of nondifferentiation that requires "the denial of strangeness and negativity" (1), traits which, in a Kristevan frame, comprise the abject; and (4) The aestheticized body emerges through the identification of abject body parts and their amendment.[3]

Extending the cultural resonance of Kristeva's *Powers of Horror*, I propose that the industry imaginary advertises *abjection* as an enduring condition that surgical practices seek to keep—from all appearances—in check. Simply put, abjection is comprised by those parts of us that we refuse, those aspects of our embodied being that we do not welcome as part of the constitution of ourselves as subjects, as part of the constitution of our identities. The abject reminds us that we are animal, mortal, material bodies, and that there are no clear or impenetrable or unbreached borders between what we are and what we reject, between what we expel and what we contain. The "actuality" of the abject body is, at the same time, a cultural development: the urgency of human abjection is implied by the institutions and interests that exist to provide for it, so that the anxiety that I feel about my body rests on psychosomatic evidence intensified by the aesthetic surgical imaginary's claim that beauty maintains psychological well-being, and that the beauty industry is, in effect then, providing good medicine. Since each one of us can be overwhelmed by the natural abjection of our bodies, a fuller theoretical and rhetorical awareness of cultural representations of abjection can perhaps help us answer the call of the imaginary more thoughtfully and powerfully. Further, the recognition that the aesthetic imaginary is a real cultural force should prompt us to view perceptions of the unacceptable body as founded not on private psychological bases, but on complex social structures and cultural repressions.

My association of the aesthetic surgical industry with the elements of an imaginary draws on Althusser and emphasizes the industry's ideological work. Following his own famous declaration that "Ideology is a 'Representation' of the Imaginary Relationship of Individuals to their Real Conditions of Existence" (162), Althusser explains that an ideology is imaginary in this sense because it represents reality while masking its constructedness, that is, its interestedness in maintaining a certain set of "facts" or conditions as real. The imaginary necessarily sets aside historical or material conditions that would disrupt the ideology's integrity or subvert its power. In its conception of body as product and patient as consumer of a future perfected image, the aesthetic surgical imaginary instances Althusser's proposition that "*all ideology hails or interpellates concrete individuals as concrete subjects*":

> I shall then suggest that ideology 'acts' or 'functions' in such a way that it 'recruits' subjects among the individuals (it recruits them all), or 'transforms' the individuals into subjects (it transforms them all) by that very precise operation which I have called *interpellation* or hailing, and which can be imagined along the lines of the most commonplace everyday police (or other) hailing: 'Hey, you there!' . . . Experience shows that the practical telecommunication of hailings is such that they hardly ever miss their man: verbal call or whistle, the one hailed always recognizes that it is really him who is being hailed. (173–74)

The aesthetic surgical industry's unique mode of interpellation, the "before-and-after" picture that shows, say, wrinkles, fat, and sagging skin replaced by a tight, lean, "new you," presents the aesthetic subject a mirror of her own abjection through a visual analogy to her own variance from the clean and proper body, which is the body in vogue. Thus, the success of industry interpellation does not really rest upon false identification or misrecognition—which are often noted as elements of the Althusserian model as it operates in advertising, in conjunction with the Marxist fascination with "false consciousness"—since the physical features and conditions its images present are believed, with good reason, to represent an actual and repellent dimension of human nature that, as Kristeva proposes, drives identification with the symbolic. Althusser's premise that everyone is subject to the hailing ideology, and that self-recognition by the interpellated subject is more involuntary than not, may be especially accurate in the case of the aesthetic surgical imaginary, since identification with abjection is inevitable and accounts for the power of the industry's appeals. Interpellation promotes transformation (e.g., Haraway, "The Promises of Monsters" 333), and in this case, may activate responses that range from consumption of the imaginary/industry's goods and services to the active refusal and reconstitution of its aesthetic. That the beauty industry profits by convincing people that their bodies are less attractive than other bodies, or altogether unacceptable, is hardly a revelation. But explicating the aesthetic imaginary as a strategic system of social and cultural representation, and elaborating a lexicon for its exposure, remains an important and incomplete project. Because embodiment, both social and personal, does feel difficult and painful much of the time, and because the industry's remedies seem to become more and more efficient and effective, the imaginary's visions of the abject body and its own therapeutic powers can seem to call to us as unmediated facts, rather than through a supervisory ideology. It is thus necessary to develop analyses that continue to "denaturalize" the normalizing force of the future perfect that the industry presents.

OBJECTIFICATION AND FALSE CONSCIOUSNESS

Feminist scholarship has, of course, begun this effort. As I will indicate more fully below, much feminist work concentrates on *objectification*, and proposes that aesthetic surgery dehumanizes and disempowers the patient, whose efforts at self-improvement lead to her objectification under the male gaze. This emphasis on the objectified female body follows from a well-documented philosophical tradition that has established the female body as inferior and disorderly. In this tradition, the female body has been excluded from the male province of the sublime—and its associations with the transcendent intellect and eternal truth—to be relegated to the category of the beautiful, subject to mutability and corruption.[4] Edmund Burke defines the beautiful—connoting smallness, smoothness, fragility or delicacy, and light— as quite distinct from the sublime, which he describes in terms of vastness, ruggedness, heartiness, and darkness or obscurity (124). Kant genders Burke's distinction by declaring that women are beautiful, men sublime: "[C]ertain specific traits lie especially in the personality of [the female] sex which distinguish it clearly from ours and chiefly result in making her known by the mark of the beautiful" (76). Burke and Kant continue a deliberation on the status of the beautiful initiated by Plato, who provides the impetus for the modern conclusion that the beautiful is an inferior aesthetic value, producing pleasing feelings but not the superior powers that describe sublimity: ecstasy, bliss, and a sense that the divine has been approached. Plato's Socrates speaks of beauty in many of the dialogues,[5] often in an effort to give it place in the physical world. *Philebus* is perhaps the most forthcoming on "the qualities of measure and proportion [that] manifest themselves in all areas as beauty and virtue": the beautiful is what pleases ear and eye, is associated with ideal proportions in the relation of part to part (good measure, symmetry), and is smooth, clear, white, simple, unified, and regular (454). For Socrates/Plato, however, the concern is not so much with beauty as a body than as a transcendent idea. It is a Platonic commonplace that all actual or material objects may be beautiful insofar as they imitate their nonmaterial archetype, but they are always inferior copies of a superior original that lies beyond the full reach and understanding of the human senses. In sum, ideal beauty is the early and long-standing philosophical solution to relativity in human sense perception and taste, and to mutability in material nature.

The aesthetic surgical industry maintains conceptions of ideal beauty that spiritualize the surgically beautified body and maintain aversion to the ordinary body. In this way, the industry continues a dominant tradition in philosophical aesthetics that feminist theorists have been working to reconstruct. Following the Platonic, neo-Platonic, and Enlightenment arguments that an ideal body is no body at all, a body freed from its materiality, the industry often presents an etherealized or disappearing body in its advertisements: the faces of aestheticized patients surrounded by halos, or with sparkling rejuvenated eyes above a nose and mouth airbrushed into invisibility, or—in a striking incongruity—with red, baggy, aged eyes set into a face otherwise bright, smooth, and youthful. Such images feature the body as a collocation of parts in varying states of transcendence, with some areas already fading from materiality or sparkling with an otherworldly glow, and others awaiting repair.[6] Beautification becomes the ascendence from the temporal realm of the beautiful to the eternal sublime, while it also reveals, under critique, the widespread pornographic representation of the female body as dismembered and anonymous (see, for example, Caputi), and also suggests the identification of transcendent beauty with the erasure of the abject body.

By the early 1990s, feminist commentary on surgical beautifying was in full swing, with strong denunciations of the aesthetic surgical industry in print, among a range of efforts to refute the oppressive idealization of the female body and reconsider entrenched aesthetic categories and values. The most influential voices of this movement, Susan Faludi, Naomi Wolf, and Susan Bordo, are largely absorbed with elaborating resistance to the beauty industry, and promote the displacement of false consciousness by critical consciousness. Feminists who give added dimension to such positions include transgression theorists who describe the power of a performative abjection (Morgan, Yaeger, Russo) and both popular (Friday) and scholarly (Davis) writers who associate beautification with the strategic development of female agency. This colloquy of voices rises up alongside the surging popularity of aesthetic surgery, and describes an aesthetics that is, by turns, defiant, conformist, ambivalent, ironic, and abject.

In this introductory discussion, I focus on Faludi and Wolf in order to establish their influential views of the objectified patient. A look at their work prepares us to consider alternative assessments of the makeover patient, as motivated by a conditioned desire for identification and community, as against the imminence of abjection. In her 1991 *Backlash*, Faludi treats aesthetic surgery among an assortment of exposés that focus on television, film, the fashion industry, advertising, national politics, and the workplace in order to show that women are being persuaded to participate in their own subjugation as part of a conspiratorial backlash against the gains made by the women's movement. In the chapter on "Beauty and the Backlash," Faludi observes that store mannequins appear to be growing ever more beautiful, primarily because real women can now approximate a mannequin's look through plastic surgery; she speaks of the "dummies coming to life" in the form of live women who go under the surgical knife (201). Such women act out of a conditioned hatred of their natural selves.[7] The aesthetic surgical industry's effort to keep in step with certain professional gains made by women initially took the form of linking women's beauty with their professional status (Faludi cites a 1988 Nivea skin cream ad that asks, "Is your face paying the price of success?" 202); later ads further manipulate women's anxiety about appearance by implying that "High achieving women can be ravaged by executive stress" (202).

Faludi argues that the beauty industry responded to poorer profits in the early 1980s by convincing women that they were ailing patients—suffering from professional stress and declining good looks. In response, the industry put an array of strategies into place in order to treat these patients: beauty became medicalized, with potions, skin injections, chemical treatments, and the rise of a plastic surgery industry that became more fully medicalized, with liposuction performed by physicians, an increase in hospital departments of cosmetic surgery, and medically prescribed and supervised liquid diet programs (203). Faludi contends that women have sometimes become quite ill from carcinogens and immunopathics (in the form, for instance, of silicone breast implants), and that many have come to associate frailty and infirmity with beauty, as displayed in the "waif look" of painfully thin fashion models.[8] She observes that the appearance of the idealized sickly woman coincides historically with the suppression of women's independence, and that the encouragement of physical vigor and vitality coincides with a culture that is more receptive to that achievement (she traces several cycles of this phenomenon in the twentieth century alone). In addition to sickly women, the beauty industry Faludi describes has also promoted images of childlike women, women in physical collapse, and subdued and silenced women.

Focusing on the female breast, Faludi argues that in 1983, the American Society of Plastic and Reconstructive Surgeons started to feature small chest-edness as an abnormality in women, and that this trend has largely been responsible for women's lack of self-esteem concerning their bodies (216). Calling breast surgery an investment and a way to enhance career goals, surgeons began offering easy payment plans, as a new component of the aggressive marketing of aesthetic surgery, with surgeons who previously specialized in reconstructive procedures advertising their expertise with liposuction and breast enlargement (217–22). According to Faludi, this propaganda worked, since by 1988, demand for aesthetic procedures had doubled, both enriching the loan industry that made surgery possible for the many lower-income women who elected it, and effecting a crowded caseload that demanded faster work by surgeons, thus increasing the risk and incidence of hemorrhage, nerve damage, and death. More breast implants meant more of their common consequences: pain, infection, clots, ruptures, scars (Faludi addresses the safety of breast implants, noting that implants may also cause autoimmune diseases, such as lupus, rheumatoid arthritis, and scleroderma, and may reduce the ability of cancer testing—mammograms—to discover cancers hidden behind the implants). Other procedures were also dangerous: liposuction had caused at least eleven deaths by 1987, and silicon facial injections had caused facial pain, numbness, ulcers, and deformities. Faludi's over-arching point is that most cosmetic procedures are vanity procedures, meaning that they are not done to improve the appearance of burn and cancer patients, but to gratify people's desires for a more perfect body.[9]

Naomi Wolf's *The Beauty Myth*, published in the same year as Faludi's *Backlash*, extends Faludi's efforts to vilify the beauty industry, and joins Faludi's book as a widely read statement that represented the feminist position to popular audiences. Like Faludi, Wolf believes that the continuously growing popularity of aesthetic surgery is part of the "beauty backlash against feminism" (252). In line with her overall position that the beauty industry teaches women to see their bodies as defective and takes financial advantage of their low self-esteem, Wolf views the aesthetic surgical industry as part of a longstanding imposition of the "medical control of women" (11), and, like Faludi, she considers aesthetic surgery as invasive and potentially deadly. She observes that by 1988, more than two million women had undergone cosmetic surgery, and that this figure represented a tripling over a mere two years.[10] Wolf ties this "willingness" to undergo invasion and pain in the name of beauty to women's conditioned acceptance of pain as a price or expectation of their gender: "Work, sex, love, pain, and death . . . [are] intertwined into a living knot at the center of female consciousness" (219). She calls female cosmetic surgery patients "man-made women" (220), and contends that "the 'ideal' is not about women, but about money" (232),[11] noting that women may become less tolerant of the pressure to "suffer for their sex," and that industry profiteers know this:[12]

> A mechanism of intimidation must be set in place to maintain the rate of growth, higher than that of any other 'medical specialty.' Women's pain threshold must be raised, a new sense of vulnerability imbedded in us, if the industry is to reap the full profit of their new technology acting on old guilt. The surgeon's market is imaginary, since there is nothing wrong with women's faces or bodies that social change won't cure; so the surgeons depend for their income on warping female self-perception and multiplying female self-hatred. (232)

Here as elsewhere, Wolf is interested in the way in which "the ideology of self-improvement" has been depoliticized, so that there is widespread blindness or refusal to see that ethics are at issue where beautifying the body is concerned: "No ethical debate has centered on the supply side of the Surgical Age" (235), she tells us.

Wolf also argues that the pressure on women to beautify is actually a matter of women's civil rights, just as people of color being pressured to look more white is a civil rights issue, but that we do not seem to make this connection: the "biological caste system" does not recognize "female identity . . . to be remotely as legitimate as racial identity" (55). She makes the oft cited argument that the aesthetic surgical industry encourages people to resolve their difficulties with an unsatisfactory body image through a rampant individualism: "The Surgical Age . . . is the American dream come true: One can re-create oneself 'better' in a brave new world. It has even, understandably, been interpreted as a feminist liberation: *Ms.* Magazine hailed it as 'self-transformation'; in *Lear's*, a woman surgeon urges, 'Voila! You are led to freedom'" (252).

Commentaries such as Faludi's and Wolf's, which feature women's oppression under the beauty ideal taking the form of surgical body modification, are influential throughout the 1990s, with Kathryn Pauly Morgan writing in 1999 that the aesthetic surgeon's knife is a sinister tool that injures rather than heals the body, a cruel accomplice in the definition of women's bodies as physically defective or deficient. For Morgan, the matter of choice concerning surgical beautifying is irrelevant, since a "technological imperative" now exists that compels social women to define their bodies according to the surgical beauty clinic's standards.[13] Morgan thus takes issue with the industry argument that surgical beautifying is another option for self-fashioning provided by new technologies whose use is, for the industry, an individual and politically neutral matter. Citing Foucault's theories of disciplinary power over docile bodies, Morgan throws into question the industry's claim that it offers relief from an unhappy body image; for Morgan, the aesthetic care of the self under the technological imperative is little more than forced compliance with the dictates of an oppressive regime. For Faludi, Wolf, and Morgan, women are rather hopelessly driven by dominant patriarchal forces to objectify themselves in order to both gratify male desire and to swell the coffers of the industry. Their assessments are reminiscent of the Frankfurt School Marxism that Marcuse voices in *One Dimensional Man,* where he acknowledges the successful corporate and governmental inculcation of false consciousness that has anesthetized mass culture, and doubts that critical consciousness will ever make much difference.

ABJECTION, AGENCY, AND IDENTIFICATION

Significantly, Morgan's focus on Foucault 's conception of power as a central motive force in Western intellectual and political history resonates not only with her view of the aesthetic surgical industry, but also with that of Kathy Davis, who voices significant dissent in her 1995 *Reshaping the Female Body* from critics such as Faludi and Wolf, who rely on top-down models of oppression for their analyses. Davis argues that a single-minded focus on women's oppression wrongly defines aesthetic surgery patients as "cultural dopes" in a ruthlessly controlling system.[14] For Davis, women who go under the knife act in their own best interests, resigned perhaps to the dominance of beauty ideals and their consequence on women's lives, but acting nonetheless in a way that will increase social approval, as well as job prospects and security. Davis argues that the aesthetic surgical patient is an active agent working on her own behalf within a system which, while it limits her options for self-fashioning, nonetheless provides rewards when she conforms to its values.

We might productively see this divergence—between commentators such as Faludi, Wolf, and Morgan, who view aesthetic patients as subject to a tyranny from whose grasp there are fewer and fewer means of escape, and Davis, who sees them as able to negotiate their position within a system of imperatives and constraints for their gender[15]—as resonant overall with the work of Foucault on power and the body.[16] In his early books—*Madness and*

Civilization and *The Birth of the Clinic*—Foucault focuses on the institutional oppression of deviant bodies, in which power is exercised by the few and the strong, who represent entrenched, prevailing institutions, on the many and the weak, who must be disciplined in terms of institutional and clinical values and regulations. However, the later Foucault, of *Discipline and Punish* and *The History of Sexuality*, views each individual within the cultural system as engaging a share of that system's available power, so long as she has internalized its principles of right and normalcy. In this model, power is not structured in terms of a perfect hierocracy:

> Power is not something that is acquired, seized, or shared, something that one holds on to or allows to slip away; power is exercised from innumerable points, in the interplay of nonegalitarian and mobile relations.
>
> Power comes from below; that is, there is no binary and all-encompassing opposition between rulers and ruled at the root of power relations, and serving as a general matrix—no such duality extending from the top down and reacting on more and more limited groups to the very depths of the social body.
>
> . . . [T]here is no power that is exercised without a series of aims and objectives. But this does not mean that it results from the choice or decision of an individual subject; let us not look for the headquarters that presides over its rationality; neither the caste which governs, nor the groups which control the state apparatus. . . . [It is] an implicit characteristic of the great anonymous, almost unspoken strategies which coordinate the loquacious tactics whose "inventors" or decision makers are often without hypocrisy.
>
> Where there is power, there is resistance, and yet, or rather consequently, this resistance is never in a position of exteriority in relation to power. (*History* 1: 94–95)

Foucault proposes that the exercise of power is active at numerous local levels, that its deployments pervade the social body and issue not just from cultural leaders and institutions, but also from each person who has internalized power's versions of good and bad, right and wrong, proper and improper, acceptable and unacceptable, normal and pathological.

Acknowledging the importance of Foucault's position here, Davis demonstrates through interviews with women in the Netherlands who were required to justify their aesthetic surgery as payable by government medical insurance,[17] that those undergoing aesthetic improvements are fully aware that beauty ideals can be oppressive, but either balance this recognition with the knowledge that beauty is an important and valued asset, or simply find that aspects of their bodies trouble them unduly, so that surgical modification seems the only solution.[18] Davis's work indicates the extent to which beauty is not a myth, but an active agent in the structure of women's lives.[19] In sum, Davis argues (and I concur) that amending the body can be a self-conscious, well-informed decision. Though objectification—as a desire and a consequence—is an element of such a decision, leaving beauty-desire at that is reductive.

In this study, I recognize that (1) *abjection* is created and sustained by the aesthetic surgical imaginary; (2) while the *state* of abjection is characterized by alienation, the *process* of abjection (ridding ourselves of the unwanted) is an act of orientation to a welcoming community, populated by clean and proper bodies; and (3) the aesthetic surgical imaginary portrays the amended body as a necessity for communal integration, while it insists that the aesthetic surgical patient is an autonomous agent. The interpellation of the aesthetic industry imaginary calls to our informed and intelligent desire for community and identification, by showing us the prospect of more perfect bodies that correspond with our best intellectual, emotional, and spiritual selves.

After elaborating Kristeva's theory of abjection in chapter 1, I describe in chapters 2 through 4 the place of abjection in the aesthetic surgical imaginary, through a range of examples that indicate the proliferation of that imaginary in contemporary popular culture. Associating the influence of the beauty industry—or as it is more generally portrayed in this century, the makeover industry—with the objectification of patients creates an impression of passivity that cannot fully explain the prevalence of the aesthetic surgical imaginary. Presuming some measure of agency at work on the patients' part, I propose that the aesthetic makeover involves the patients' conditioned self-objectification of abject body parts or features in the service of a conditioned desire to identify with the society of clean and proper bodies. The interaction of objectification, abjection, and identification is encouraged by the aesthetic surgical industry/imaginary; however, the desire for identification is transposed to the desire for autonomy, so that industry-generated desires become understood and justified as I-centered.

Throughout, I draw from representative advocacies that constitute the phenomenal visibility, accessibility, and popularity of turn-of-the-century aesthetic surgery: a wide range of trade books published between 1998 and 2001, which function as industry advocacies; advertisements for aesthetic surgery appearing in 1999–2001 in the *Palm Beach Post* and other Palm Beach County, Florida, publications, which represent the industry to one of its largest constituencies;[20] official publications of the American Society of Plastic Surgeons (ASPS), the American Society for Aesthetic Plastic Surgery (ASAPS), and the International Society for Aesthetic Plastic Surgery (ISAPS); and 2001–2002 television episodes of *A Personal Story*, which documents an aesthetic surgery success story every weekday on cable television's The Learning Channel, through a thirty-minute narrative that presents the before-and-after lives of actual patients. These representations of the aesthetic surgical industry at the turn of this century are definitive pieces of a hypertext with a tremendous multimedia reach, into so many magazines, television features, advertisements, and web pages; thus, they do not constitute the full extent of the industry's presence in our lives, but do tell a consistent and representative story of its appeals, and do constitute the lived reality of a middle-aged academic feminist who writes from Boca Raton, Florida, one of the makeover capitals of the world. In chapter 5, I expand my focus on the clinical medical practice of surgical beautifying to describe the translation of an aesthetic imaginary into popular, preceptive philosophies for controlling difference and disorder, as they are presented by celebrity self-help guru Oprah Winfrey and by the American Association of Retired Persons' official publication for the aging, *Modern Maturity*. Oprah, the most widely known and watched television personality at the turn of the century, and *Modern Maturity*, the most widely circulated magazine, both focus consistently on the rejuvenating virtues of the psychophysical makeover, defining and legitimating a culture in which "makeover" has become an increasingly popular name for the normalization of the self around procedures and prospects that are tied up with body image and related forms of abjection.

It is to this larger cultural imaginary—which attempts to dream and talk its way out of temporality, fragmentation, specificity, and difference—that Kristeva and other postmodern psychoanalytic theorists repeatedly allude. [21] By focusing on the relationship of abjection to makeover culture in these media, I wish to extend critiques that have already been issued by feminist theorists, social scientists, and medical historians, and to contribute to the formation of a more fully cultural perspective on psychoanalytic theories of abjection. But more pointedly, I wish to recontextualize abjection: it has been understood primarily as an impulse that constitutes the unwanted other, the dismembered. However, beginning from the premise that abjection is the objectification of the repulsive body prompted by the conditioned desire for society, I locate abjection in the aesthetic surgical imaginary's appeal to membership, to identification, and attempt to understand it as an insistently individual impulse that is really a group project, while I admit that the elimination of the variant body is a serious ethical problem and an actual impossibility.

CHAPTER 1

Abjection

For Julia Kristeva, the intolerable, or abject, body leaks wastes and fluids, in violation of the desire and hope for the "clean and proper" body, thus making the boundaries and limitations of our selfhood ambiguous, and indicating our physical wasting and ultimate death. In her view, human and animal wastes such as feces, urine, vomit, tears, and saliva are repulsive because they test the notion of the self/other split upon which subjectivity depends. The skin of milk, for instance, puts one in mind of the thin skin membrane that defines the borders and the limits of the physical body; because human skin provides only a relatively flimsy and easily assaulted partition between the body's inside and the world outside, this milky reminder disturbs our distinctions between outside and inside, I and other, moving us to retch, and want to vomit in an acute attempt to expel the scum from our being (Kristeva, *Powers of Horror* 2–3). As Elizabeth Grosz observes, "Abjection is a sickness at one's own body, at the body beyond that 'clean and proper' thing, the body of the subject. Abjection is the result of recognizing that the body is more than, in excess of, the 'clean and proper'" (78). The abject body repeatedly violates its own borders, and disrupts the wish for physical self-control and social propriety. We disavow our excretory bodies because they are signs of disorder, reminders of the body's ambiguous limits (its leaking from multiple orifices), and of its ultimate death: "Such wastes drop so that I might live, until, from loss to loss, nothing remains in me and my entire body falls beyond the limit—*cadere*, cadaver" (Kristeva, *Powers* 3).[1]

Kristeva's theory of abjection originates with her distinction between the semiotic and the symbolic in *Revolution in Poetic Language*. Here, Kristeva claims that language is the outgrowth of certain drives and desires that are somehow "presymbolic," or we might say, prerepresentational. These drives and desires are *semiotic*, and their life exists in the place or space of the *chora*. Kristeva adapts the concept of the *chora* from Plato's *Timaeus*, a dialogue between Socrates and Timaeus about the nature of material existence, where the *chora* is usually translated into English as "receptacle." This passage from the *Timaeus* indicates that for Plato, the *chora* is the place out of which *being* develops:

> For the moment, we need to keep in mind three types of things: that which comes to be, that in which it comes to be [*chora*], and that after which the thing coming to be is modeled, and which is the source of its coming to be. It is in fact appropriate to compare the receiving thing to a mother, the source to a father, and the nature between them to their offspring. (Zeyl 50d)

The *chora* is thus related for Plato, as for Kristeva, to the maternal. It is the place where the developing "thing" (in Kristeva's case, a child) is "nurtured." In human relationships, this nurturing consists of the mother responding to the child's needs (that is, her heterogeneous energies and drives), and directing both the expression and the satisfaction of those needs. The child experiences hunger, alertness, and drowsiness, all of which are answered by the mother, who suckles the child, talks to her and makes faces at her, cuddles her as she drifts into sleep, and so on. Though the child hears words spoken around her, she has not yet been initiated into formal language, but experiences the world mainly in terms of rhythmic or sporadic movements, sounds without pre-scribed sense, feelings of pleasure or pain whose origin or cause is indefinite. Language is already beginning to develop in this semiotic phase of existence, since certain patterns of being in the wake of sound are imposed on the future speaking subject. She hears certain sounds—words—repeated around her, and registers a variety of tones and vocalizations in her surroundings, and they may gradually begin to correspond to states of bodily feeling, for instance, her mother's soft whisper as she enjoys the warmth of being at the breast and filling her belly. The child is thus beginning to experience correspondences of sounds, words, desires, and feelings; a world is beginning to take form, but it is still a world that is largely dependent on the mother and her body for its maintenance and definition.

The semiotic phase is followed by a rupture, which Kristeva thinks of with reference to Lacan's theory of the mirror stage. Lacan writes of a time in a young child's development when she recognizes herself in a mirror for the first time. "What's that?" the child thinks. "Why, that seems to be me, since when I move, the image moves; I see where I begin and end, so I am an individual, and that means that I am not continuous with my mother's body, but separate from it." This introduces the child to the idea that not only is she a person separate from the mother and from objects in the world, but also that persons and objects can be reflected back to her through representation, through images or figures that depict or describe persons and things, but which are not identical with those persons or things. This is the point at which encoded words become central. Because the child had not previously been aware of the world as a representational place of persons and objects, she had no connection with naming. But now, as she begins to cross from the semiotic—in which language was all movement, rhythm, sounds without referent—into the symbolic—in which language points at persons and things and gives them a public meaning—she needs to know the names of persons and things in order to communicate with others. This moment of drift from the semiotic toward naming—toward becoming participatory in a signifying system—is for Kristeva a "thetic phase" (98). Kristeva depicts a young child in a state of language in which the semiotic and the symbolic are cooperative: the sound the dog makes—"woof-woof"—becomes the signifier for the dog, and the dog is called "woof-woof" by the child. This is a thetic moment, in which the child "attribute[s] to [an entity] a semiotic fragment, which thereby becomes a signifier" (43).

A significant difference between Plato's concept of the *chora* and Kristeva's use of it is that Plato goes on to describe the *chora* as a kind of nonthing with reference to being:

> [W]e shouldn't call the mother or receptacle of what has come to be . . . either earth or air, fire or water, or any of their compounds or constituents. But if we speak of it as an invisible and characterless sort of thing, one that receives all things and shares in a most perplexing way in what is intelligible, a thing extremely difficult to comprehend, we shall not be misled. (Zeyl 51b)

Plato finds the *chora* to be a kind of cipher, a receptacle whose only function is to contain being, and being's source is simply the father. For Kristeva, the *chora* is not characterless. Though it belongs to an arrangement that is prior to symbolic representation, it is nonetheless a place or space of significant activity, rather than an empty receptacle. The child's early intimacy with the mother's body is not only itself a kind of language, defined as it is by patterns of sound and movement, but it is the ground of all symbolic, or social language; it is what makes language acquisition possible.

Bearing in mind Plato's reduction of the *chora,* or place of the mother, to nothing, we might be able to see how it is that Kristeva's work is revolutionary. She is interested in the variety of ways in which semiosis and *chora* have been forgotten or repressed in and through a symbolic language that we might say is aligned with the Platonic view of the *chora.* The symbolic order, as it has taken shape in global culture, is an acculturated language that often simply acts as, sees itself as, a substitution for bodily instincts. The semiotic relationship to the mother, which had a less external relationship to the world—constituted as it was largely by the child's drives and their private articulations—begins to be lost as the child enters the symbolic. And Kristeva proposes that much of the symbolic language in which we engage has the effect of establishing and maintaining us in a relationship with the not-Mother, who becomes the other, and we inhabit a world too radically external to the mother.

However, Kristeva tells us that the semiotic and symbolic languages are not discontinuous or discrete from one another:

> These two modalities—the semiotic and the symbolic—are inseparable within the signifying process that constitutes language, and the dialectic between them determines the type of discourse (narrative, metalanguage, theory, poetry, etc.) involved; in other words, so-called "natural" language allows for different modes of articulation of the semiotic and the symbolic. (24)

The symbolic bears traces of the semiotic, of the mother tongue, of the "various processes and relations, anterior to sign and syntax . . . [which are] previous and necessary to the acquisition of language, but not identical to language" (96). So, the activity of the symbolic is not without what has largely become the pre-conscious or unconscious semiotic, even as it is a transformation, or sublimation, of it.

Kristeva's contribution (in *Revolution in Poetic Language* and elsewhere) to efforts by philosophers and linguists to see the relationships among language, mind, and culture is to posit the semiotic processes as elemental to art. *Revolution* treats Mellarme and Lautreamont, showing how radical poetic language simultaneously incorporates and violates conventional grammar, syntax, and meaning.[2] For Kristeva, a revival or recognition of semiotic language creates the possibility for breaking out of the constraints of a law-governed symbolic order, to create art that violates conventional rules, and "murders" proper meaning. Dreams and fantasies continue to remind us of the presence of the semiotic in our mental life, as do artistic and poetic productions.

Kristeva's argument for the retrieval of the semiotic strains or energies through a reading of poetic language is revolutionary, since a rigid insistence on the priority of the Symbolic Order in symbolic language[3] not only makes linguistics a failed or partial enterprise, but also stifles creativity and silences the body. If the semiotic state is a time in which the child's bodily instincts are given more expression, more play, the child who has entered into the s/Symbolic condition finds language exerting its regulating influence the more forcefully on the bodily instincts, so that the psychology and behavior of the child begin to be shaped in the image of the Symbolic.[4]

In the mirror phase, the child begins to turn toward that formative figure in her life that represents the symbolic order, which Kristeva and Lacan both associate with The Law of the Father, though Kristeva also associates the father with love, and this is another way in which she qualifies or complicates Lacan. As Plato indicates, the source and model of becoming "real" in the world is understood as the father, in contrast to the receptacle within which early dependence takes place, which is the mother. Thus the sensual and maternal semiotic world is largely supplanted by the symbolic world, which involves turning toward the rules of language, of expression, of codified behavior, of rules and regulations, of conventions.

The mother is left behind—abjected, Kristeva says—and with her all elements of the self that threaten or violate codes of behavior and discursive expression. She is thus separated from "the clean and proper subject," whose body is regulated by codes of good social behavior, and repressed in and through symbolic language. For Kristeva, everything that is filthy or disorderly or uncivilized is in the same "place" as the left-behind mother, in the realm of the abject. Like the semiotic, then, the abject is also what is suppressed and repressed within and through symbolic language. So this horror of the abject body is, as with the semiotic, linked with the body of the mother, but with an even more radically other mother than that addressed through the concept of the semiotic. One of Kristeva's interests is the ways in which the necessary abjection of the mother—our separation from her in order to become individualized, to take objects, to enter language, to become good citizens of the family and the social world—is mistranslated into the abjection of women in general, who are reduced to the maternal function.

The abject is, as we are beginning to see, a more radical alterity than the semiotic: it refers to the power of the mother's body over the child, a power that is not perfectly brought under the control of the Symbolic or Paternal Order. The mother's body represents a threat, and in her essay, "Stabat Mater," Kristeva demonstrates how the threat of the mother is brought under control, domesticated in the myth of the Holy Virgin, mother of Christ. She argues that the Christian virginal representation of the maternal satisfies the aims of the (phallocentric) Symbolic Order because the virgin is the impossible ideal up to which all women are held, and serves as mother, daughter, and wife to the Holy Son. Kristeva herself disrupts this narrative in the course of the essay by inserting stream-of-consciousness soliloquies about the experience of maternity. For Kristeva, the pregnant woman—as opposed to the figure of immaculate conception, the erasure of women's sex—is a figure of the doubling of self into other, and the eventual splitting of the self into the other, a figure that bespeaks both the identification of the self with the other, and the negation of self in the other that makes the recognition of the other possible.

The symbolic order mostly succeeds in abjecting the mother, repressing her power, as Kristeva indicates in "Motherhood According to Giovanni Bellini":

> It is as if paternity were necessary in order to relieve the archaic impact of the maternal body on man; in order to complete the investigation of a ravishing maternal jouissance but also of its terrorizing aggressivity; in order somehow to admit the threat that the male feels as much from the possessive maternal body as from his separation from it—a threat that he immediately returns to that body. (*Desire in Language* 263)

Abjecting the mother goes beyond simply recognizing the need to separate from the mother, and enter language, because it is also motivated by the Paternal Order's fear that the mother's body is a devouring body. The semiotic mother, we recall, does participate in the process of imposing patterns and order on the life of the infant, and is, in that sense, an arm of the Symbolic Order.[5] The abject mother is an archaic mother because she is, as Kelly Oliver says, "pre-identity, presubject, preobject" (57), and in that way, utterly noncompliant with the clean and proper bodies regulated by the symbolic order: "Kristeva gives [in *Powers of Horror*] a [further] example of the revolutionary effect of the repressed maternal in language. [Here,] the authority of our religion, morality, politics, and language comes through the repression of horror [of the abject body]. . . . Our culture is founded on this horror" (101). As Oliver says, "The Symbolic can maintain itself only by maintaining its borders; and the abject points to the fragility of those borders" (56).

PAIN

We might view each socially abject body as analogous to the mother who is both the object of waste and, with her menstrual blood, its distinctive source;

each is a castoff unless and until it reenters the cultural logic that articulates health and beauty, a reentry advertised by the aesthetic clinic. Each experiences, to borrow a concept from David Bakan, *telic decentralization*. In biological terms, telic decentralization describes the action of living cells that divide and differentiate in the service of organismic growth. The teleological, or purposive form of the body is understood as both its drive toward integrity and its capacity to function in specialized ways. Bakan conceives of the human body as composed of various loci of organization, or multiple teleological centers, including *disease tele* and *constructive tele*. Disease tele are of the lowest order, because they do not work for the common good of the organism, and do not communicate with the constructive tele. Bakan also posits a psychical form of telic decentralization, making use of the Freudian tripartite mind, in which the psyche as a whole splits into the id, ego, and superego. In a healthy organism, the three psychic telic centers communicate with one another, working toward the greater good of the organism. This form of telic decentralization accounts not only for the mind's complexity, but also for its degeneration into incoherence or fragmentation: certain experiential trauma may be repressed, producing neuroses and psychoses which result from a lack of free-flowing communication among psychic centers.

Bakan applies the concept of telic decentralization beyond the individual body and mind to the relation between individual persons who are divided through their bodies from the larger social body. Here, Bakan focuses on physical pain as he discusses this separation: "Pain is the burden of the organism separated out of the larger [social] telos . . . the occasion when one is ripped from union into a condition of physical individuality" (64).[6] For both Bakan and Elaine Scarry—who adapts a number of Bakan's concepts in *The Body in Pain*[7]—the ego moves to externalize, or make alien, the source of its suffering. Significantly, Kristeva says, "The abject has only one quality of the object—that of being opposed to *I*" (*Powers* 1). The alienation of pain (from the self) and the objectification of pain (as diagnosis) are psychotherapeutic counterparts for the sufferer seeking relief. Diagnostic objectification, the means by which the sufferer brings pain into the external, and potentially curative, world of cause and effect, is also the means by which she psychologically makes pain alien.

The point of substantiating pain is to cancel it. Intervention is the point at which sufferer and nonsuffering community meet, an event that must take place in order for the sufferer to retrieve her social connectedness: "A cry of pain coming from one person may, at the very least, evoke in another an effort to help the person who is in pain; and thus pain is also a means of returning to the *dominion* of the social telos" (Bakan 61, emphasis added). (Alien) pain divides the sufferer not only from her own (pained) body, but also from the (supreme) pain-free population for whom pain is a deviant and unnatural condition. Reestablishing oneself among this group—becoming "recentralized"—requires not only that the sufferer make her pain known, but also that the pain be eliminated (Bakan 61). To objectify pain is thus to stamp it out in two senses: to give it tangible shape, and, potentially, to extinguish it. In other words, she must lose her suffering parts. Though Bakan has compassionate healing in mind when he speaks of pain's obliteration, it is also true that the obliteration of pain removes the sight of suffering from "the dominion of the social telos."

Through their developing recognition that the aesthetic surgical industry needed justification on medical terms, as a service in relief of pain and suffering (and thus committed to the "recentralizing" of its patients), aesthetic surgeons had found by the mid-twentieth century a viable way to define their enterprise as a respectable and necessary medical practice by claiming that body beautification acts as a kind of psychotherapy. As both Sander Gilman and Elizabeth Haiken demonstrate, the aesthetic surgical industry owes what legitimacy it now enjoys to the reciprocal ideas that dissatisfaction with the body causes unhappiness, and that this unhappiness will lift when the patient's body is beautified.[8] Gilman points out that the birth and development of psychoanalysis roughly coincides with the establishment of modern aesthetic surgery, and observes an inverse relationship between surgical aestheticizing and psychoanalytic therapies:

> The basic premise of aesthetic surgery rests on the simple reversal of the psychosomatic model that underlies orthodox psychoanalysis. For the psychoanalyst psychic 'misery' is written on the body as physical symptoms; for the aesthetic surgeon, the 'unhappiness' of the patient is the result of the physical nature of the body. (*Creating Beauty* 13)

The industry's continuing use of this "somatopsychic" dynamic, in which altering the body affects the mind, comes forward in its specialized use of the term "psychosurgery" to indicate the ultimate destination of the surgeon's scalpel (see, for example, Engler 30–32). Pruzinsky's and Edgerton's well-documented 1990 observation that "[t]he only rationale for performing aesthetic plastic surgery is to improve the patient's psychological well-being" (217) indicates that by the beginning of the 1990s, better mental health had become the industry's raison d'etre.

The estrangement of persons from the body parts that cause psychic affliction—in obeisance to a social telos that requires bodily sacrifices in the name of wellness—is active in an aesthetic surgical industry-imaginary that decentralizes the targets of its appeals, encouraging prospective patients to see the body as an inventory of parts, one or more of which produce suffering, and which must thus be erased. On the whole, the aesthetically unmodified body is posited as an unfortunate deviation from the beautified bodies considered integral to a well-functioning relationship between the individual and her society. This is to say that the felt alienness of the unsatisfactory body parts to the sufferer's ego is always tied up with the very ways in which the body is understood by a community whose language allows only for an abjecting model.

COMMUNICATION AND EXPULSION

The disarticulation of mind and body, and body from self and society, centralized for Kristeva in the abject mother, is brought forward as a problem for feminist psychoanalysis by Teresa Brennan, who would answer Freud's "riddle of femininity"—involving women's greater depletion of sublimating energies following from the Oedipal conflict—through a focus on his theory of the mind as an economic, individualized, autonomous structure. Brennan argues that subjects are not autonomous entities, but exist in a lived relation to and exchange of psychic energies with other subjects. The "imprint" of one's own psychic energies—desires and demands—is always potentially transferable to the other, and this dynamic defines the process of masculinization and feminization. Brennan returns us to Freud by establishing the body as structuring a language fundamental to psychological subjects. She argues, in phylogenetic terms, that beings in utero speak a language that is both logical (allowing for a communication with flesh that facilitates growth and development), and affective (in a dependent relation with the flesh of another). Physiological growth involves a chain of interconnected events that progresses from one state to another:

> Presumably facilitating connections are basic to the language of the flesh, which has to be logical, in the sense that one thing connects with another in a way that facilitates growth. . . . [L]ogical thought, the connections made through words, is a kind of mimesis of a hypothetical original form of communication which was both mental and physical. (223)

Yet the constructive power inherent in human language suffers because at some point language becomes disconnected from the affective feeling that once made up a part of its character.

This process has, for Brennan, gendered significance, so that the male subject's language typically disengages from its affective part, displacing it onto an other, while it is the female subject that typically accepts this imposition, and loses some capacity for transforming feeling into speech. This imposition has devastating results for women:

> Moreover it is a divorce that suggests that affects, or emotions, are the confused residue of the original logic of the flesh, left over and muddled up once they have been subtracted from that original logic through speech, after the subject has been cut off from that fleshly logic, or castrated. (224)

Masculine practice displaces or disposes of affective feeling onto the woman, needing her, but as a kind of wastebasket, so that she becomes the castrated affect. Woman's relegation to affect and body remains, however, somehow unnatural to the logic of the body in Brennan's construction, inimical to the communicative potential of body language.

Brennan qualifies the constructionist jump to the social, not in order to argue that social conditions do not inform psychological subjects, nor that change is possible because social conditions are largely constructed. She looks at features of reproductive embodiment that may predispose us to certain psychological patterns, the understanding of which, she argues, can help us to more effectively modify social conditions. Brennan focuses on the body as a pre-conditioned language: there is a biologically realized tendency to connectedness that the body acts out, and that the body imitates. That tendency, on a biological level, is essentially constructive: it makes life, it assures growth. For Brennan, physiological growth is logical: a chain of interconnected events that takes us from one state to another. Acknowledging Lacan's positing of a psychological world that is structured as and by language, Brennan wants to locate this in the body, in the flesh:

> If, as I have argued, some part of the structure of language is based on an original form of intra-uterine communication, then the question had to arise as to why language works in ways that either facilitate or hinder connections. Presumably facilitating connections are basic to the language of the flesh, which has to be logical, in the sense that one thing connects with another in a way that facilitates growth. This suggests that logical thought, the connections made through words, is a kind of mimesis of a hypothetical original form of communication which was both mental and physical. And if, as I have argued, the word can be turned in certain directions, a turning hinged on its connection with a

visual image, affects, and motor activity, then this direction will affect the ease with which connections are made. This must be so, given that the image can lock a word inside hysteria (femininity). In masculinity, the outward forceful projection of image and affects should allow those words to flow more freely, but at the price of a divorce from affective feeling. (223–24)

In this model of body and communication, the network of connections is purely constructive. There is no address to the problems of decay and dying, to the presymbolic semiotic that is illogical and eventually abject, or to the fact that growth entails waste.

Therefore, to Brennan's answer to the riddle of femininity, I would add that the wasting of the flesh is also an aspect of the body's life, activating a symbolic that both resists abjection and associates it with the female body. Understanding this initially involves acknowledging that the growth of the body entails the expulsion—the abjection—of its nonnutritive contents. Just as the body is an articulate organ that fosters communication in the service of growth, this growth—and later, mature health—of the body requires the expulsion of what would otherwise contribute to sepsis. As natural as it may be to have communication among cells in order to promote growth, and an intrauterine "conversation" with the cells of the mother's body upon which the fetus depends, that fetus is also expelling waste through the placenta into the mother. Thus, our growth and health entail not only a certain constructive logic, but also the expulsion of the contents of decay and death. This is the way we first know what it is to expel into and onto an other.

One could say that the two forces or efforts—communication and expulsion—work in tandem, as a physiological unit, which sets up the psyche to attach certain significances to the body's activity. During intrauterine life, it will simply be the case that the subject perceives itself as an articulating body that requires an other into or onto whom it may displace its waste product. Later, it will be the woman/(m)other who becomes the conscious receptacle of choice, at first due to her perceived connection to the child's body, and later due to bodily associations with abjection: menstruation, pregnancy, lactation, excess of adipose tissue. She is, as Kristeva has argued, the fleshly language before it becomes sanitized and masked as the logic of the symbolic order. Maternity is, in this sense, the opening of one's body to the act of being shat into or upon, and interestingly, this dynamic is reflected in the male/female sexual parts.[9]

What I press here, in association with Brennan's propositions about the divorce of mind from feeling that defines the conflict between masculine and feminine, is that disarticulations of language and body also occur within the frame of reference of the body whose corporate nature is always called into question by the body without firm borders. For Brennan, the divorce of affective feeling from the masculine needs correction, since disarticulate communication corresponds with disarticulate psyches. For me, the same is true; however, to Brennan's emphasis on masculinity's rejection and displacement of affective feeling, I would add rejection and displacement of the body that wastes, and propose that the wasting body is any body that does not exhibit the cultural symptoms of health, including ill health associated with being the weaker sex, race, age group, or shape.

While I agree with and admire Brennan's bold move to read flesh in tension with our fears about essentialism, arguing that this scruple has kept us from really theorizing the body, I remain suspicious of psychoanalytic insights that involve prerational subjects, and see these models as not necessarily phylogenetic and infant developmental absolutes, but as figures or narratives that allow us to enter into a critical dialogue about the displacement of the abject body onto women. The question is how to reconfigure these biological mechanisms in thought and representation so that social life does not mirror their meaning in fixed terms, so that woman does not internalize as her obligation the imprint of masculinity's desire and demand to abandon its fleshly nature.

TRANSGRESSION, IDENTIFICATION, AND COMMUNITY

Through this discussion of Kristeva, Bakan, and Brennan, I recognize abjection—both as it originates with Kristeva and as it is implied in the other theorists' focus on the problem of the disarticulate body—as part of an intensely personal state of being. At the same time that abjection is part of the individual's struggle to live as a pain-free self, it is also, as I have stated at several points, a metaphor for the process of maintaining the social body. Kristeva's counterposition of the abject against the Symbolic, with the Symbolic understood as the articulate social order, indicates that the individual in a struggle against her own dissolution is also in a struggle against social alienation.

Kristeva's consistent focus on the individual's struggle against abjection has provoked some criticism of her as apolitical (c.f., Leland), and it is the case that Kristeva is more interested in the self than in selves. Therefore, relocating Kristevan abjection as a social and communal process requires some measure of adaptation, so that we are able to see the body *in* society as the corporate and collective social body, and understand the psychobiological struggle against dissolution as analogous to the struggle for social and communal identity.

Those who have attempted to adapt Kristevan abjection to social action have focused on the struggle *against* social and communal identity, and adapted the abject body as a figure of transgression. This approach is fully warranted, since, in her monstrosity, the abject woman stands apart from both those who are oppressed by the beauty ideal and those who strategically conform to it. She has informed feminist typologies at least since the advent of Cixous's 1975 "Laugh of the Medusa." Countering Freud's conspicuous display of gynophobia and its parent neurosis, androcentrism, Cixous recasts Medusa as a smiling and powerful woman, and rings in a postmodern pantheon of new embodiments, for instance, Heilbrun's androgyne, Daly's crone, Haraway's cyborg. These contend with traditional constructions of the female body as a weak and beautiful ornament disqualified from intellectual and plastic distinction, and offer visions of prodigious bodies with subversive minds, aesthetic hybrids whose nonconformity with feminine ideals betokens their power.

Patricia Yaeger and Mary Russo[10] focus explicitly on aesthetic transgression by envisioning abject women who violate two of the principal categories of philosophical aesthetics, the sublime and the grotesque. Abjection enters their work largely as the Kristevan concept describing body waste and leakage (menstrual blood, withering flesh, excrement), with emphasis on the social positions of those outside the borders of what is "clean and proper." Though Yaeger and Russo do not write explicitly about aesthetic surgery, they are thinking about conformity with the cultural beauty ideals to which the contemporary aesthetic surgical clinic is highly responsive. For both, the abject woman becomes a subversive trope of female liberation: she speaks an alternative, disruptive language, immersing herself in the significances of the flesh, becoming willfully monstrous as she defies the symbolic order. She abandons her oppressive confinement to the category of the beautiful, reforms her association with the grotesque, and contests her expulsion from the sublime. Yaeger and Russo conceive of an aesthetic—unlike the aesthetic surgical imaginary—that revels in abjection, viewing its pressures on the body as symbols of a womanist power, and reforming an aesthetic of the body that issues from misogyny and somatophobia.

Yaeger's 1992 essay on the "*maternal* sublime" proposes that women refuse the weak category of the beautiful, and look, instead, to the grotesque and the sublime to serve a feminist aesthetic. Observing that "the world of the beautiful can be treacherous for women" (5), Yaeger notes that this measure of women's value is instrumental in keeping them in invisibility, paralysis, and confinement.[11] In traditional aesthetics, the sublime is more powerful than the beautiful, tied up with ecstasy, force, and movement. Sublimity bespeaks "the noumenal power of the once-inferiorized [self]" (9), but is "unavailable to the spatially constricted woman" (6).[12] But the sublime woman can involve herself in "joy and vaunting," a self-glorying that refuses "constriction and miniaturization" (6). Women refuse the beautiful and embrace the sublime by emphasizing their own powers of generation, specifically their maternal power. Asking whether "there is room for women's reproductive labor in the smoke-filled rooms" of the Romantic sublime (9)—associated with conversion, spatiality, and personal power—Yaeger argues that maternity, despite its traditional connection with the grotesque, can belong also to a sublime poetics. She adapts Edmund Burke's view that *terror* is the whole basis of sublimity, positing the birthing woman as a type of grotesque that sublimely terrifies. Yaeger notes that the mother's body has often been defined as defiled, ruptured, and unclean—*abject* in Kristevan terms—and thus argues that the mother's body registers the dread prerequisite to sublimity: abjection conditions the embodiment of robust motion and gore.

Russo's 1995 *Female Grotesque* also conjoins grotesque and abject in the development of a new aesthetic. Emphasizing "grotesque performance" for women, Russo admires Amelia Earhart's aerobatic stunting for its refusal of conventional femininity. The history of literary and artistic representation, as well as the history of public and political discourses, reflects and reinforces the imperative that women keep themselves small and unseen, that they neither take up too much space in the world, nor make spectacles of themselves. As a subversive alternative, Russo prefers that women make themselves prodigious and visible, that they seek majesty, and so disrupt long-standing definitions of the ideal woman as restrained and diminutive. A grotesque performer like Earhart practices philobatism, or the will to be suspended in mid-air, defying her groundedness within and through traditional femininity. The grotesque performer, because ugly and aberrant according to conventional culture, refuses the imperative that she stay beautiful and domesticated, and seeks the heights of self-fashioning with reference to a body that does not obey prescribed limits. For Russo, Earhart's stunting is both a model of female exceptionalism and an instance of woman as sideshow object, simultaneously demonstrating and rebuking her cultural status as a monstrous body.

Noting that the grotesque body is always a social body, Russo rehabilitates the identification of the grotesque, noted by Bakhtin, with "the lower bodily stratum and its associations with degradation, filth, death, and rebirth" (8). She argues that traditional aesthetics has devalued the grotesque body, preferring the classical body, which is "transcendent and monumental, closed, static, self-contained, symmetrical, and sleek . . . identified with the 'high' or official culture of the Renaissance and later, with the rationalism, individualism, and normalizing aspirations of the bourgeoisie" (8). By contrast, she identifies the grotesque body, "open, protruding, irregular, secreting, multiple, and changing," with the social rebirth and reformation called for by "the non-official 'low' culture or the carnivalesque" (8). Russo suggests that the ideals upon which Western subjectivity has relied for the construction of its values and knowledge—normalcy, purity, transcendence—constructs itself in opposition to the qualities with which the grotesque is associated: the abnormal or perverse, the filthy or tainted, and the earthly or grounded. The grotesque is also the Freudian uncanny, because Western subjectivity refuses through its ideals precisely what cannot be refused: the mortal corporeality that incites human fears.

Russo argues that the female grotesque and the abject woman are related, since the maternal body has long been associated with the grotesque. The "cave—the grotto-esque" (1) she notes, may be compared to the cavernous anatomical female body. Russo makes this connection through Bakhtin's "senile, pregnant hag," and through "a vein of nonacademic 'cultural feminism'" that valorizes the earth mother, witch, crone, and vampire, arguing that these figures "posit a natural connection between the female body (itself naturalized) and the 'primal' elements, especially the earth" (1). In addition, she maintains that the locating of the grotesque in art "as superficial and to the margins" suggests "a certain construction of the feminine" as equally devalued and disenfranchised (6). The maternal partakes of the uncanny to the extent that it threatens "always to monstrously reproduce," to double as conjoined self and other (18); the philobatic imagination, too, "operates, at different stages, both *within and away from* the maternal body" to the extent that subjectivity is formed through the simultaneous love and repudiation of the mother (36). Russo recognizes that "it is an easy and perilous slide from these archaic tropes [woman as earth, cave, witch, and vampire] to misogyny [since] all the detritus of the body that is separated out and placed with terror and revulsion (predominantly, though not exclusively) on the side of the feminine—are down there in that cave of abjection" (20). However, she would exploit the association in the direction of a liberation strategy: the woman as "monstrous" defier of social norms.

The association of physical and cultural disfigurement with power remains, in the visions of Yaeger and Russo, and related celebrations of the monstrous in Daly, Haraway, and Cixous, largely an intellectual and figurative process, calling for a reconstituted female aesthetic imagination that may, to the extent that concepts form practice, activate actual social change. As I have noted, Kathryn Pauly Morgan calls for more direct intervention when she proposes that we have aesthetic surgery as a form of protest. She calls for a corps of feminist radicals who go under the knife to make their noses bigger, have fat injected into rather than sucked out of the body, add facial wrinkles, and create more pendulous breasts. Like body piercing and tattooing, which were once identifiers of protest and refusal, uglifying aesthetic change could become subversive, undermining "the power dynamic built into the dependence on surgical experts who define themselves as aestheticians of women's bodies" (162). However, Morgan recognizes that her proposal is utopian, and that "refusal and revolt exact a high price" (163) within the aesthetic surgical imaginary. Thus, she blunts the general criticism that Lynn Segal gives in *Why Feminism*, proposing that formulations of the feminine "in terms of its seditious 'Otherness'" (50) can seem pitifully oblivious to current social and political realities.

It is those realities to which I will turn in chapter 2, which offers an introduction to the global influence and ideals of the aesthetic surgical imaginary, which normalize our conceptions of the clean and proper body. I will return to the monstrous feminine toward the end of this study, to affirm the power of what I call "inspired abjection" to maintain the possibility of radical alternatives in the midst of these powerful normalizing forces. But my primary interest in the following chapters will be the role of abjection in social and socializing processes, rather than as the mark of the anti-social. In this connection, it is the case, as Kenneth Burke and others have pointed out, that the creation of society is largely a rhetorical process, enacted through *identification*. For Althusser, identification is the recognition of oneself as hailed, as an interpellated object. Notwithstanding his value to our critical lexicon for understanding the operation of the aesthetic-surgical imaginary, Althusser's stress on the power of the hailing ideology encourages the stress on objectification that also characterizes feminist top-down models of the persuasive power of commercial beauty advertisement. The Althusserian model does provide us a representative anecdote for how the appeal of the imaginary is operationalized, but does not—as much Marxist theory does not—understand people who accede to the appeal as much more than dumb objects.

Kathy Davis has moved us toward a fuller recognition of aesthetic surgical patients as willful and intelligent agents, but has not provided a full explanation of the motivating desire that would explain why, as chapter 2 will show, so many millions are amending their bodies. Developing this explanation means explicating the relationships among objectification, abjection, and identification as elements in the process of creating and maintaining one's social life. In this process, objectification refers to the commodifying of the body, not only in the sense that Faludi and Wolf develop, of women reduced to the objects of male desire, but also as self-objectification that identifies—in complicity with the aesthetic surgical imaginary—the parts of the body that should be amended, its abject objects. Identification is most usefully understood in the terms established by Kenneth Burke, as motivated by the desire for *consubstantiality*, or "shared substance." Consubstantiality is, for Burke, a "compensatory" motive that arises out of the human aversion to division. We would, for Burke, rather act together than apart, "and in acting together, [people] have common sensations, concepts, images, ideas, attitudes that make them *consubstantial*" (*Rhetoric* 21). Feminist rhetoricians have pointed out that Burke's stress on identification and on the human aversion to division can lead to the valorizing of social cohesion and the discouragement of protest and nonconformity (Ratcliffe). This is, indeed, a problem that we cannot ignore, especially insofar as identification may be the central motive for acceding to universal beauty ideals. At the same time, identification (as the desire for consubstantiality) has the explanatory power required to move us away from an overly simple conception of the aesthetic surgical patient as an object. Instead, we can come to see this patient as embedded in a vast network of industry appeals that are largely visual, and which bring into view the clean and proper bodies that are purported to result once abjection is complete, once those features and parts that are not consubstantial with an emerging universal ideal are amended.[13]

CHAPTER 2

Normalizing the Body

The abject does not negate. Rather, the abject excludes.
—Julia Kristeva, *Powers of Horror*

The "clean and proper body" is a condition for our ability to be articulate subjects in the social world; however, the orderliness and stability of this body are always under threat, and always illusory: "The more or less beautiful image in which I behold or recognize myself rests upon an abjection that sunders it as soon as repression, the constant watchman, is relaxed" (*Powers* 13). A form of body repudiation, abjection is also a critique of such repudiation, confronting the impossibility of achieving its own desire. Present in the inseparability of body and waste, abjection finds no objects whose repudiation can permanently save it. This is what Kristeva means when she says that abjection has "properly speaking, no definable *object*" (*Powers* 1). The wasting body is an incessant reminder that the subject abides under her own radical splitting, into disruption, psychic disturbance, the dissolution of boundaries, limits, identity, and flesh. Because the corpse is the waste (the wasting) from which the subject cannot in the end separate, she lives in a constant state of failed aversion from her own atrophy. Here is not cause for some abject "song of myself" that disavows repression and celebrates the wasting body, but a call for the acknowledgment that abjection is always present, and foundational to cultural conceptions of beauty.[1]

The abject permits an increasingly sophisticated makeover industry to be simultaneously preoccupied with and isolated from the very set of conditions that has occasioned and fostered its growth. Just as the body requires a process of abjecting its waste product in order to survive ("wastes drop so that I might live" [*Powers* 3]), so does the symbolic "eliminate" some of its own content in order to thrive, and to know what it is (not). Thus, the abject is always being articulated (though negatively) by and within the systems that seek to dispel it. This accounts for the repressed concerns that the aesthetic surgical industry has about its own legitimacy as it recasts the differing body into the mold of a new purification.[2]

The Scar

Beautifying the body can often be achieved only by scarring it, sometimes extensively, and always, when incisions are made, permanently. Kristeva associates invisibility, abjection, and scarring in her discussion of Oedipus, who blinds himself in order to reinforce "the boundary that wards off opprobrium," leaving a "scar taking the place of a revealed and yet invisible abjection. Of abjection considered as invisible. In return for which city-state and knowledge can endure" (*Powers of Horror* 84). Here, Kristeva presents the scar as the mark of social alienation, while it is also the means by which the society of clean and proper bodies is purified and maintained, as a symbolic that governs both political order and self-knowledge. In this connection, the scars inflicted by the aesthetic surgical industry, which are, because all surgical procedures are elective, also self-inflicted by the patient, mark the point where the visible and abject body once existed.

Self-identification that corresponds with membership in the restored social order is impossible for Oedipus because he is wholly abject, and must shut himself, through self-inflicted blindness, completely away. For the aesthetic surgical patient, there is a synecdochic relationship between the offending body part and the whole self, which, as we will see in chapter 3, leads to the association of a face lift with psychological, spiritual, and social regeneration. Following the narrative of the aesthetic surgical imaginary, cutting away or reshaping an undesirable part results in a made-over person who can interact more fully and successfully in society, and who is able to identify herself more confidently as a member of the social body. The self-inflicted scar, implemented by the industry, thus indicates the point of objectification (of the offending part), abjection (through its amendment), and integration of self-image, self-knowledge, and social integration.

One of the specialties of the aesthetic surgical clinic is scar revision, which involves making "better" scars (less contrastive with the skin) from those that were created by injury or nonaesthetic surgeries, such as the emergency repair of facial lacerations. The same surgeons who revise scars are also in the business of creating them: they beautify by cutting—to tighten skin or reproportion body parts— but leaving wounds that often cause weeks and months of pain, swelling, and bruising. Seeming to recognize the paradox in this incision of the clinically healthy body under the claim of healing and improvement, and struggling to stress its role in ensuring the integrity of the body that is so crucial to both mental and spiritual health, the industry devotes great rhetorical energy to negotiating the tension between beautification and scarring.

Some of the most extensive discussion of scarring occurs in descriptions of breast augmentation procedures, which number among the most popular of aesthetic modifications (increasing from about 20,000 procedures per year in 1992 to over 200,000 in 2000). The most hidden, but most palpable scar resulting from a breast implant is the "capsule," a hard wall of tissue that forms around the silicone-covered, saline-filled implant, which may cause a tugging sensation, pain, and a palpable stiffness or hardness. But there is also the external scar, a problem that absorbs much of the compendious standard clinical reference, *Surgery of the Breast: Principles and Art* (Spear), which devotes rather obsessive attention, through extensive description and multiple case histories, to the advantages of the inframammary scar, drawn just above the crease of the breast to allow for insertion of the implant, and thus well hidden. The industry recognizes some advantage and disadvantage in all breast scars, and presents them to the lay public as a menu of choices, suggesting the possibility of a sort of customized scar, the scar that is right for you. In this connection, aesthetic surgeon Alan Engler devotes a chapter of *BodySculpture* to asking his lay audience, "Which Incision [is right for you]?" and provides a rather enthusiastic tour of the secondary questions that inform this one: How well hidden must the scar be? How do you define "hidden"? (Clothes on? Clothes off? Lights on? Lights off?) How much tension will the scar suffer from work or exercise? (this will affect its healing, and thus its appearance), and so on. For Engler, the axillary incision (under the armpit) was once an excellent camouflage for patients getting implants, but today, with more women wearing sleeveless clothes (exercise outfits and the like), it may be that the periareolar incision (on the lower perimeter of the nipple) is most hidden, preferable even to the inframammary incision above the crease of the breast, which, as Engler warns, may be exposed if the patient is lying down, or if a bathing suit top rides up (55–59).

The breast procedure involving the most dramatic scarring is the breast lift, or mastopexy, which requires cutting away the nipple and the skin below it and sewing the breast back together to produce a scar often referred to as a "lollipop." Metaphorizing the mastopexy scar into a piece of candy accords it a perverse erotic sweetness that may discourage repulsion, at the same time that it heightens the clinic's urgency to reconceive its damage. Recognizing that scarring is an inevitable and worrisome side effect of most surgeries, and exerting control over its vicious, abject connotations, industry advocacies feature scars in a positive light, presenting them as marks of the surgeon's competence: "One of the main skills of plastic surgeons is controlling scar formation" (Gelfant 29). Typical assurances that attempt to minimize the visibility of scarring, present it as evidence of industry power over abjection, and maintain the integrity of an aestheticized body that governs self-image, are represented in Marfuggi's, *Plastic Surgery: What You Need to Know Before, During, and After:*

Liposuction: "You will have incisions measuring three to six millimeters where the canula was inserted. . . . Scars, though present, are usually placed where they will be most inconspicuous." (46)

Tummy tuck: "Scars, though permanent, usually fade over time and are placed in areas where they will be easily hidden by your underwear. You can expect it to take from nine months to a year for scars to mature. A skillful surgeon will make incisions where they are easily hidden." (59)

Breast lifts: "Mastopexy scars are permanent; however, they are generally positioned so that you can wear strapless tops and low necklines." (80)

Blepharoplasty (eyelid surgery): "The incisions follow the palpebral fold of your upper eyelids. . . . [The incisions] tend to heal so well that they are often described as 'disappearing.'" (99)

Rhinoplasty: "Standard incisions are placed inside the nasal airway." (117)

Otoplasty (usually the pinning back of the ears): "Because the incision is usually made in the back of the ear, concealment is not a major concern. Let your hair grow before your operation to assist in camouflage." (128)

Facelifts: "Ideally, incisions are positioned where they will be hidden by hair or fall into natural skin folds." (140)

Forehead and brow lift: "The scalp incision leaves a permanent scar, which is totally within the standard hairline where it will be hidden. If you do lose your hair, it will be seen." (147)

Hair restoration: "In general, scars are hidden by the hair." (185)

Male breast reduction: "Most commonly, the incision is placed in the lower half of the areola where . . . [it] will usually heal in an inconspicuous manner." (195)

Significantly, all of these statements feature the scar as a kind of benevolent volitional force that, with the aid of the surgeon, is readily concealed or tends toward its own erasure.[3] In a summary that encourages patients to appreciate the quality of their scars, Gelfant tells us, "Incisions in the upper eyelids, the lips, the groin, and the armpits are especially good, while incisions in the centre of the chest, upper back and the upper outer arm are particularly prone to bad scars. The face, in general, tends to form good scars, if they are properly planned" (30).[4] Surgeons advertise their talent for making incisions whose damage will be either hidden behind clothes, or will gradually fade into ghostly "thin, fine white lines" (Ganny and Collini 106), rather than remaining ghastly slashes.

These scars, clean and proper as they are in the industry's representation, speak, however, for the articulation of abjection within the system that seeks to dispel it, and its refusal to disappear. The eventual fading of "good" scars into whiteness presents them as signs of redemptive trauma whose marks no longer signal the eruption of the unwanted body, and though they remain less than ideal, good scars also evince the bloodless purity of the body whose borders have been sealed, whose spirit within is secure. The scar, however, confronts the aesthetic surgical patient and industry with an abject appearance that has merely been repositioned—literally, hidden under clothing, buried in an armpit, concealed behind an ear, but also figuratively, as the sign of the instabilities and contradictions that cast doubt on the social and cultural positions that physicians and patients seek to occupy. Though in one sense the scar protects the borders of the body, keeping the I from leaking out into the not-I, it is, through the eyes of the aesthetic surgical imaginary, also wild tissue, an indication of the body's tendencies toward disorder. Like the sagging breast that tells my age, or the bulging fat deposits that resist diet and exercise, the aesthetic scar is the improper body in a state of uprising against beautification. As Gilman observes, scars "are the shadow presence of what the patient wished to hide" (*Making the Body Beautiful* 48–49); what she would hide are the places where desire and the desirable are breached, marks of the eruption of discontinuity that provokes "horror and abjection" (Tucker 1).

BODY LOATHING

As the *healthy* body becomes the corollary of the *beautiful* body (note the now well-established practice in most department stores of stocking "health and beauty" supplies in the same section, thus teaching us that you can't have one without the other), medical treatment becomes the corollary of aesthetic treatment. This correlation expands the practice of medicine, to include both the surgical breast lift to enhance self-image and social vitality, and colorectal surgery to remove a vicious, deadly cancer. In both cases, medicine intervenes in an enmity between the desire for a "good" (read clean and proper) body and the determination of a "bad" one. The aesthetic surgical industry-imaginary did not create this split between the imaginary whole body and the fragmented body of difference, between the good body and the bad body: it has long been elaborated in the cultural and institutional discourses of religion, philosophy, and medicine. The industry does reinscribe, however, an understanding of the abject body as what should and can be sacrificed, so that unity of self and consciousness can prevail or be restored. To this end, aesthetic modification participates in a reinscription of the body as an object of suspicion and antipathy that resists our efforts at identification with its insistent unruliness. The industry reinforces a splitting in the psyche by dividing the body into two, into what we may call the abject and the "glorified" body, seeking to eradicate the former so that only the latter informs the subject's understanding of self. This division gives rise to a discourse of abject body loathing that can become especially fierce in some of the most enthusiastically promotional books.

The enfranchisement of body loathing coincides with an encouragement of proactive behavior that is less directed at whether to undergo a procedure, than at choosing what procedures to undergo. Bingo Wyer surveys the possible types who might consider beautification:

> So who are you? And how would somebody who knows you really well describe you? . . . Make a few notes, then see if you can spot several shared traits with the following groups:
> "I'm okay." We all know people with a balanced self-image who tend to work well with others, even if they are extremely reserved and quiet. Their daily lives are varied. Emotional outbursts are rare. They do not fear spending time alone, nor are they phobic about social gatherings. They are members of some community—a workplace, family, or the town in which they live. These types may be bothered by a physical characteristic that they would like to improve or change.
> "I'm okay, but . . ." The line between this group and the former is almost imperceptible; both share many similar traits. However, for this group, the bothersome feature gains psychological importance over time. Fat thighs, for example, keep them from going to the beach with friends. Occasionally, they may perceive rejection when there is none. This low self-esteem, however, does not govern their daily lives. After cosmetic

surgery, the majority enjoy good results. Their adjustment may be slower; building confidence usually involves time.

"I'm okay, but help!" Invariably this group is made up of teenagers or young adults. They have a particularly high awareness of an appearance flaw. These defects may be real or imagined. For some, their looks seem to have changed overnight. Protruding ears, a disproportionate nose, or bad skin begin to erode self-esteem. When teasing and ridicule ensue, the young person's confidence may not adequately develop. Cosmetic surgery can prevent the emotional turmoil brought on—whether real or imagined—by the rejection of others.

"I'm okay, but I love my corporate earning power!" . . . These cosmetic surgery candidates achieved significant career success early on. Now an equal number are keen on staying at the top; they view cosmetic surgery as a tool to help extend corporate tenure. (9–10)

Here, we see that aesthetic surgery is for the well-adjusted, the maladjusted, and the overachievers. It is not for those who are delusional or in the midst of emotional crisis (Marfuggi 6; Burgess 15); it is, instead, for a collective majority populated by reasonable, intelligent, relatively healthy people (Burgess 14): the appeal to such traits both maintains a rather large population of potential candidates and encourages readers to identify themselves with the good sense that seems to characterize the best elective patients.

Aesthetic surgery advocates Charlee Ganny and Susan Collini feature dissatisfaction with one's appearance as a source of distress, even as they feature surgery as the obvious solution:

> A flaw with your face, including those caused by age, is serious psychological business. . . . So why shouldn't you correct any other facial flaw that has been causing you inner pain for too many years of your life? Stop the emotional hurting. Go see a doctor for a consultation and find out what is involved in fixing it. (127)[5]

Sarnoff and Swirsky tell us, "A multitude of problems—from unsightly leg veins to disconcerting acne scars, from impulsively etched tattoos to disfiguring port-wine stains, from puffy and tired-looking eyes to embarrassing stretch marks affect . . . [more than 120 million Americans] from infancy to the nineties" (2). Henry and Heckaman encourage us to dread "the cold, cruel reality of morning light [that reveals the sagging and wrinkling of our] naked sleepy face[s]" (xi–xii), while Gaynor tells baby boomers to disdain their heavy "thighs, droopy faces, and lines between their eyebrows that make them look angry all the time" (1). Ganny and Collini insist that "Contemporary American society fully accepts and, in fact, *expects* us to correct crooked teeth, crossed eyes, or even jug ears" (127, emphasis in original). Imperfections become deformities, and efforts to live with one's disorderly body become delusions, as in "The Ten Biggest Lies Women Tell Themselves":

1. "I like having small breasts."
2. "I don't look my age."
3. "I don't mind looking like my mother."
4. "This nose gives my face character."
5. "I earned these wrinkles and am damn proud of them."
6. "I'll lose ten pounds—after the holidays."
7. "Makeup can hide the bags under my eyes . . . the scar on my cheek . . . the mole by my nose . . . the lines around my mouth."
8. "My husband loves the way I look."
9. "I *can* flatten my tummy; I just need to start going to the gym."
10. "With the right clothes, nobody notices . . . my thunder thighs . . . my bubble butt . . . my midriff bulge . . . my bingo arms . . . my chicken neck . . . " (Ganny and Collini xvii)

The desire for a consubstantial relationship with the advertised social body, in which loathsome parts are at worst hidden and at best cut away, is activated through self-loathing. The objectification of the self-as-other (abjection) is made easier, and increasingly mandatory, by the widespread media presence of the aesthetic surgical imaginary, which not only inculcates a ready lexicon for describing the unwanted, both in colloquialisms such as "bingo arms" and in popular technoaesthetic terminology such as "microdermabrasion, but also features a television and web-based visual pantheon of both deformities and corrections. These provisions bring the abject body and the clean and proper body so fully and so constantly under the public gaze that the desire for identification and consubstantiality is impossible to ignore and difficult to resist, as the numbers of those who elect aesthetic surgery rise dramatically.

Industry Success

The American Society for Aesthetic Plastic Surgery (ASAPS) reports that 8,470,363 million people elected to have their features altered in 2001. The removal of wrinkles and fat were favorite pursuits, judging from a 2356% increase from 1997 (to 1,600,300) in Botox injection treatments to temporarily paralyze facial muscles that define crow's feet and other face lines; and from the top popularity of chemical peels (1,361,479) that use glycolic or trichloroacetic acid to remove the blemished surface skin layer, microdermabrasion (915,312) to remove surface skin layers through the sanding effects of micron crystals, collagen injections (1,098,519) that fill in pocks or wrinkles, sclerotherapy (557,856) to destroy varicose veins through the injection of an irritant solution that induces scar tissue formation and vasoconstriction, laser hair removal (854,582) for the light-activated disabling and delay of hair growth, and liposuction (385,390) that liquefies fat and sucks it out.[6] Breast lifts and augmentations, facelifts, and rhinoplasty continued to draw large numbers, for a combined total of 571,352 (American Society 3).

Scarcely any part of the body remains untouched in the aesthetic practitioner's menu when we consider the availability of all these procedures, along with abdominoplasty (tummy tuck), buttock lifts, calf implants, chest implants, cheek implants, chin lifts, earflap modification, earlobe augmentation or reduction, eyebag surgery, eyelid surgery, fat injections, forehead lifts, lip augmentation, lip reduction, lower body lifts, male breast reduction, penile enhancement, pectoral implants, permanent makeup, scalp reduction and scalp expansion (for male pattern baldness), scar revision, thigh lifts, upper arm lifts, varicose vein removal, and even labiaplasty that is not part of a sex change reconstruction, but rather an effort to customize the appearance of the vagina (Kamps).

Aesthetic medicine is a widely visible industry, with well-established national and international professional organizations,[7] thousands of information and advocacy pages on the web, and a print and media presence that keeps it before the public on a daily basis in the form of ads, magazine and newspaper features, and television newsmagazine and talk show self-improvement advice and exposés. We can identify some of the properties explicated here in many centers of culture: the indirect or accessory interpellation of aesthetic surgical subjects also takes place at the most general level through the privileging of youth and beauty that proliferates and intensifies as contemporary culture becomes more and more saturated with body images, more pointedly in the marketing of cosmetics, nutrients, and pharmaceuticals for the elimination of various symptoms of aging, and in particular and hugely popular media products aimed at controlling the abject body.

The accessibility of industry information on aesthetic surgery has been dramatically affected by the growth of Internet resources: websites created by individual health professionals, clinics, hospitals, and professional organizations provide descriptions of procedures, pricing, physician referral, statistics, histories of the profession, advertisements of new products, position papers by and for professionals, calendars of professional meetings, trends, chat lines, and financing plans. Prospective patients can select a physician and a procedure, as well as secure a loan, without ever leaving home.

The web pages for each of the major professional organizations stress a statistical recent history that verifies the desire for and acceptance of aesthetic surgery, so the claim that more than eight million people went under the aesthetic knife in 2001 can be read as both an indicator of a really substantial and increasingly popular business, and an advertisement for the association that culls the numbers. The ASAPS summarizes a 2002 consumer survey of "1000 American Households," which tells us that 57% of women and 53% of men approve of aesthetic surgery (18). This endorsement runs especially high among baby boomers, 63% of whom say they approve. Such figures, coupled with the ASAPS figures that advertise a 304% increase across all aesthetic surgical procedures performed since 1997 suggest that majority approval should indeed be in place, and that aesthetic surgery is losing some of the stigma formerly associated with it as a vanity fix for those with low self-esteem. In the ASAPS "Household" survey, 79% of American women say that they would not be embarrassed to reveal having had a surgical operation to others. It is not surprising that the highest approval ratings are associated with the most privileged group: high income, white Americans who are most likely to elect surgical procedures that are exclusively aesthetic have become both the evidence for the success of the global aesthetic clinic and the target of the suasive power of the numbers.

Claiming that the desire for beauty is original with human beings and urging conformity to long-standing Western beauty ideals, the industry creates a majority politic for its practice, not only relating patient celebrations of successful surgical outcomes, but also reviewing the sociological and psychological research that verifies what Sarnoff and Swirsky call the "halo effect" to describe the importance of good appearance to social and professional life (15). Faced with the repeated, commonsensical observation that "For the majority of people, looks matter" (Sarnoff and Swirsky 1) and a media culture in which "plastic surgery is everywhere" (Loftus 1), those not possessed by beauty desire, defined in terms of the aesthetic procedures that are popular and possible, would seem to be operating outside the laws of natural and cultural selection.

The urgency to market the virtues of fitting into the general public has given rise to a mythopoetic grandeur in the advertisement of aesthetic surgery, suggestive of the extraordinary power of the surgeon to restore youth and beauty, but intended to trade in the centers of normalcy. As writer and surgeon Alan Engler suggests in this biographical apologia, surgical beautifying is for young and old alike:

> On a hot August day I was walking through a department store. It was during a heat wave—the type where everyone is advised to stay indoors and seek shelter in a shopping mall if air conditioning is not available. As I headed for the exit I passed through the cosmetics department. Walking toward me was a woman in her 40s and a girl, presumably her daughter, about 15 years old. As they approached, I saw that the girl was becoming a bit wobbly on her feet. I moved nearer to them just as her eyes rolled back and she started to faint. I jumped forward, caught her as she was falling, and lowered her onto the ground. Her mother became hysterical and blurted out that her daughter hadn't eaten a thing for lunch. After determining that the girl had simply fainted and would be okay, I reassured her mother. I asked for some water. A store employee brought out an atomizer of designer water, which I sprayed onto the girl's face. She opened her eyes and looked up at the ceiling. Her mother, now calmed, turned to me and, noticing my beeper, asked if I was a doctor. I nodded. Next she asked what kind of doctor I was. "Actually," I said, "I'm a plastic surgeon." At that point the girl, apparently revived but still lying flat on her back, lifted her head up sharply and asked, "Oh wow! Do you do liposuction?" The mere mention of plastic surgery appears to have spurred her recovery. (8)

Here, in a place where people take refuge from ordinary discomforts (August heat that makes our bodies swelter) and browse the indicators of cultural normalcy (a climate-controlled exhibition of skin fashions), "plastic surgeon" acts as a magic word, raising the sufferer. The damsel-in-distress motif is evident: the doctor happens to be "passing through" when the pressures of suffering—heat, hunger, and the unruly body—call him into action. He catches the falling, fainting girl, hears her mother's confession, dissolves the parent's hysteria, and revives the girl with water blessed by the beauty industry. He then restores the girl's vitality, not with nutrition, nor even psychotherapy, but with the prospect of liposuction.

In an irony unacknowledged by Engler, the girl is transformed into a more intensely enthusiastic and happy person by the excited imagination of having the material that supplies her body's energy sucked out. It is not at all clear that she is a candidate for liposuction, and the implication is that the prospect of that procedure has redemptive power for us all, that the very presence of aesthetic surgery and its agent can activate new psychic health, and cure us from the crisis of possessing ordinary bodies susceptible to mutability and social othering. The girl's dramatic awakening is Engler's proof of the aesthetic surgical industry's imprint on the contemporary, collective American psyche. This aesthetic surgical imaginary proffers an updated incantation of provision for the body that is remarkably effective precisely because it so often calls to us from our own abjection. That "call" echoes in the cosmetics department where Engler's girl faints, where alertness to one's variance from ideal beauty is engaged at every step.

UNIVERSAL BEAUTY

The contradiction between the advertisement of aesthetic surgery as a mass movement and as a distinctive exercise in individual choice is further evident in the universalizing of the ideal body. As so many critics have recognized, the exteriors that the industry recommends and effects conform to an aesthetic conventionally associated with the canonical Western art of antiquity and are part of what Francette Pacteau refers to as "metaphysics of universality" (14). Though industry advocates often make the argument that the clinic is not rigid in its determinations of what features constitute beauty, acknowledging that beauty ideals change over time and across cultures, and making the case that beauty ideals are not strictly Caucasian ones, the use of familiar Western artworks corresponds with the advertisement of body types that maintain dominant models of the beautiful body. Advertisements often picture classical representations of beautiful women, such as Venus or Aphrodite, and thus deliver the message that 36C breasts and smooth, tight skin render one the living version of a goddess. Though aesthetic surgical patients are endowed with the power to make choices among options (for example, breast size), the argument for a body that is "classically contoured" predominates. Benjamin Gelfant represents at some length the industry's conformity to time-honored models:

> Many plastic surgeons have continued in the classic search to define beauty and have used the classical canons of beauty, as described by Albrecht Dürer and Leonardo da Vinci and others, to aid in shaping the facial bony features to give an overall appearance of beauty. The argument is made that these proportions have universal appeal, and are seen implicitly in the forms of many beautiful things in nature (such as the spirals of sea shells) and in classically beautiful architecture such as the Parthenon. We respond to these portions in the faces and bodies of individuals we consider to be attractive or beautiful. Balance and harmony

provide a sense of completeness and stability, freed from visual tension and distortion. The Greeks believed that all beauty was based on mathematics and that beautiful objects could be analyzed by numbers. For them, a form such as a rectangle with sides of 1:1.6 was aesthetically the most satisfying. Unfortunately, absolute numbers are of uncertain value when trying to determine nose size and shape on a small thin face or large round one. (78–79)

The argument here is unapologetic for its obeisance to classical aesthetics, positing "universal appeal" as the ground of its own visual value system. As Gelfant's comments suggest, in addition to supporting physical and sexual dimorphism—conforming women to the appearances of fertility, and creating strong chins, noses, and calves in men—the aesthetic surgical industry tends to universalize Caucasian features as preferred. Speaking of equal proportions among the three parts of the face; well-aligned foreheads, lips, and chins; noses and upper lips at 100–110° angles; eyes separated by one eye's width; and heads measuring the width of four eyes across (79), Gelfant remarks that certain "overall facial shapes . . . would be considered unattractive, in any culture" (79), and cites rhinoplasty as one procedure for those who feel "ethnically conspicuous" (61).[8]

A cross-cultural perspective informs industry histories that locate the beginnings of aesthetic surgery in the Middle East and in rather unconvincing but nonetheless assertive statistical claims of increasing multiethnic participation by professional organizations such as the American Society of Plastic Surgeons: "Cosmetic surgery is on the rise for minorities too. Hispanics represent 10 percent of total patients, followed by African-Americans (7 percent) and Asian Americans (4 percent)" ("Plastic Surgery Today" 1). In carefully understated efforts to address the small percentage of Asian Americans that enter the aesthetic clinic, several trade books categorize "Asian eyes" as an aesthetic problem. Richard Marfuggi advocates the full Westernization of the Asian face in a markedly neutral and detached tone, attributing the existence of Occidental blepharoplasty to patient demand, but then pressing further possibilities for facial Westernization by recommending a nose job:

> The most common cosmetic procedure requested by Asians is blepharoplasty to give their faces a more Western, or Occidental, appearance. This is achieved by creating an upper eyelid fold. . . . Often Occidental blepharoplasty is combined with cosmetic rhinoplasty to augment and elevate the bridge of the nose, also contributing to a more Western appearance. (110)

Wyer acknowledges the criticism that attends the availability of and demand for Occidental blepharoplasty, but finally recommends to Asian patients an aesthetic of "balance" that seems to involve modifying more than the eyes, within a general implication that attendance to the multiple elements of one's "total look" should be every patient's concern:

> Asians who explore cosmetic surgery should carefully consider how subtle dimensions might be added to the face while maintaining their standards of balance and beauty. Asians, like minorities and all prospects, should seek a total look that is aesthetically pleasing. (42)

Perhaps the subtlest recommendation for Occidental blepharoplasty comes from Alan Gaynor, who simply shows before and after photos of an Asian woman, uncaptioned, at the beginning of his chapter on eyelid procedures (140). All of these trade authors reinforce the industry attitude revealed by Eugenia Kaw in her study of Asian American aesthetic surgery candidates, which concludes that the industry continues to evaluate Asian features as flat, sleepy, dull, and weak. One Asian woman Kaw interviewed recommended eventual eyelid surgery for her daughter, then twelve, because, as the mother put it, "I think that having less sleepy-looking eyes would help her in the future with getting jobs" (174). Offering a counterpoint to the desire for Westernized faces, surgeon Jean Loftus concludes her brief and clinical description of Occidental blepharoplasty with a rather unlikely alternative: "It is possible to convert a Caucasian eyelid into an Asian eyelid by surgically disrupting the attachments between the muscle and the eyelid" (77). In an implicit apology for the industry's devaluation of the non-Western face, she offers an eye for an eye.

In another uneasy moment in the advocacy of the Westernized face, Gelfant qualifies his observation that people do not want to appear "ethnically conspicuous" through a rather extensive acknowledgment that the current preference for full lips represents the tendency in the fashion press to photograph models of "mixed European and non-European racial heritage," who represent "a concept of beauty which does not necessarily reflect the classic canons" (70). The discussion then quickly reverts to an appreciation for European standards, however, pressing the term "Paris lip" to describe a Brigitte Bardot pout that complements the beauty of fuller lips (74). The introduction of Bardot, already long past her stardom when the fashion emphasis on full, Africanized lips first emerged in the 1980s, reveals some subtle urgency for a Eurocentric referent.[9]

Many commentators have observed that the multiple alterations of black pop star Michael Jackson's appearance in the 1980s and 1990s represent the aesthetic surgical potential to replace a race-specific body with one that is racially and ethnically indeterminate[10] and to ambiguate gender with the design of his soft, effeminate face. At the same time that this rather extreme case departs from the industry tendency to feature gender conformity and to prefer Caucasian features, in what amounts to a general denunciation of race and gender ambiguity, it also illustrates the industry urgency to evade the abject body by keeping it constantly under the scalpel of adjustment. As Susan Willis has noted, the aesthetic of transformation represented by Jackson entails a denial of difference, wherein distinction is displaced by infinite seriality: a "chain of simulacra" that preserves the body as a commodity fetish while it features race, gender, and age as "surgical rather than cultural identities" (1001-02). Jackson's serial identity changes become conventionalized in industry advice that patients begin aesthetic modification in their twenties with rhinoplasty and breast augmentation and undergo regular changes through every decade, keeping a lifelong schedule of face lifts and tummy tucks that deliver one's appearance away from its genetic and chronological distinctiveness, make its history and origins invisible, and limit variance to the inventory of proportions and procedures that are clinically viable.[11]

Sander Gilman observes a current shift in the cultural understanding and representation of race that has been prompted and informed by a new sensitivity to racialism, or racial discrimination, proposing that Jews, in particular, are "seen as an ethnic or religious cohort rather than a racial one. [So that] the anxiety of visibility is no longer keyed to the Jewish nose" (139). For Gilman, we tend to root discrimination today more in lifestyles than in body types. He says, however, that "one is still anxious about being seen as too Jewish" (139), and this anxiety prompts many to seek rhinoplasty each year. As Elizabeth Haiken notes in *Venus Envy*, the current tendency to question racial motives for aesthetic surgery may mean that those motives have been recategorized and subtilized by elective patients, but nonetheless persist (209–27).

The industry line on ideal beauty was strikingly evident in a 1999 radio discussion and debate between Elizabeth Haiken and Scott Spear, professor and chief of plastic surgery at the Georgetown University School of Medicine. Spear responds to Haiken's suggestion that people worldwide have been conditioned to associate physical beauty with Western European looks by acknowledging that each race has its own beauty standards (preferring particular sorts of eyelids and cheekbones and chins), then following with the assertion that there are elements of beauty universally recognizable as such: "There is true beauty . . . whether we're talking about sunsets, mountain scenes, or human appearances, there are faces and bodies that are in and of themselves beautiful" ("Cosmetic Surgery"). Thus, he at once denies participating in racial effacement, and suggests that the self-fulfillment promised by aesthetic surgery emerges from certain stable, invariable standards. There is also in this attitude antipathy to the racial body that matches the industry's antipathy to aging: the preferred self to which the skin should conform is not only young, but white.

Progressive political agency is, of course, not in line with the aesthetic tradition that the surgical imaginary reveres and which has traditionally served to reproduce existing class, gender, and race relations within societies (Hein and Korsmeyer, Brand and Korsmeyer). Industry rhetoric (consciously and unconsciously) maintains that surgical beautifying is a nonideological act and therefore, outside of concerns over societal inequities. But at the same time, it preserves the conservative virtue of a homogeneous society by arguing that surgical beautifying can make people equal to their better looking cohorts—reducing difference and bias—and allow them to take control of their abjection, so that they are the more liberated from its claims.

Thus, the aesthetic surgical industry is both remarkably progressive in its development of technological approaches to body modification, and remarkably conservative in its conceptions of the elements of beauty. Here at the beginning of the twenty-first century, when cultural, racial, and gender diversity have become watchwords in the West, the advertisement of aesthetic surgery—often voiced by surgeons who represent the membership and standard views of large professional organizations such as the American Society for Aesthetic Plastic Surgery—preserves conceptions of beauty that are anything but diverse. In the contest between essentialist conceptions of human nature and official appreciations of cultural diversity, nature may seem to be losing on a number of fronts, as the acknowledgment of cultural difference becomes routinized in venues that range from the literary canons taught in our schools and colleges to the composition of the president's cabinet to the array of contestants in the Miss America pageant. However, whether or not such examples represent a really genuine and salutary challenge to beliefs in natural, race-specific beauty, strength, and intelligence ideals, the aesthetic clinic continues to advertise the return to an ideal nature and suggest that variations from the ideal comprise an inventory of physical imperfection.

Warrants for aesthetic surgery tend to fall into four categories: (1) the desire for beauty as central to the history of human consciousness; (2) the primacy of beauty in the natural world; (3) the importance of beauty to social and professional achievement; and (4) the equation of beautification with normalcy. All four coincide in most industry advocacies.

The contemporary beauty industry is, in its self-conception, the culmination of a long history of healing and reconstructive efforts that were always subtended by the desire for beauty, and have led to a present in which that desire is, more than ever, connected to happiness and success. Both trade books and industry histories trace beautification procedures back to ancient Egypt, often citing the Smith papyrus from circa 4000 BCE, which, we are told, speaks of methods for healing wounds and softening scars that are concerned with aesthetic effects.[12] In *Beauty and the Beam*, the circa 800 BCE restoration of severed Indian noses, the repair of syphilitic noses in sixteenth-century Europe, and the technical advances in the late nineteenth and early twentieth centuries provide touchstones suggesting a timeless desire for physical beauty that culminates in the present era,[13] comprising a compact history which, in a few sweeping sentences, takes us from "the Ice Age [when] most people only lived to the age of sixteen" to the turn of the twentieth century, when "people were so absorbed with raising large families and working to put bread on their tables that they hardly noticed as the years raced by and old age abruptly descended," to today, when "the average life span has now increased to eighty years [and] both men and women have begun to change the traditional concepts of middle and old age" (Sarnoff and Swirsky 1). Legitimated through a history of desire and its fulfillment by a once primitive but always evolving aesthetic industry, ultimate claims that today's youthful seniors suffer more than ever before from the disjunction between inner goodness and vitality and exterior corrosion suggest that longevity, cultural advancement, and aesthetic technologies have grown through the centuries into a significant complicity.

In his history of the International Society for Aesthetic Plastic Surgery, Ulrich Hinderer concludes that the Society has helped the aesthetic surgical industry to achieve its major goal of the twentieth century: to "become a respected field of medicine, represented by a responsible body of plastic surgeons" (1) who have risen above the specialty's association with unethical "beauty doctors."[14] The American Society of Plastic Surgeons' "History of Plastic Surgery" speaks to this distinction from its first paragraph, according the profession the ethos of an ancient and traditional medical practice that addresses an inherent human need:

> Mankind's essential nature entails self-improvement. . . . Because human beings have always sought self-fulfillment through self-improvement, plastic surgery—improving and restoring form and function—may be one of the world's oldest healing arts. In fact, written evidence cites medical treatment for facial injuries more than 4,000 years ago. Physicians in ancient India were utilizing skin grafts for reconstructive work as early as 800 B.C. (1)

By paralleling the individual's desire for surgical beautification with "the pursuit of peace with his or her neighbors and more efficient means to work," and worrying that without such pursuits, human "progress would stop," the ASPS history represents the only medical profession with an advertising and advocacy campaign that associates global harmony and development with good looks.

In this spirit, Sarnoff and Swirsky offer a sweeping cultural history of beauty, reaching back to the biblical Eve: "No doubt vanity—and its counterpart, self-consciousness—first arose when Eve donned her fig leaf in the Garden of Eden and perhaps adorned her face with the pigment of berries. Ever since, people have continued to place a high premium on enhancing their appearance and looking younger" (16). Besides the implicit but unintended linking here of beautifying with shame at the body's animal characteristics, this mythical account of the aesthetic clinic's foundational moment aids the notion that the burden of aestheticizing the body falls primarily to women. Thus, the more oppressive dimensions of mythic heterosexuality depend (as revealed, for instance, by Bataille in *Erotism*)[15] upon the woman enhancing her sexual difference from men, that is to say, enhancing her beauty, which is the sign of that sexual difference.

Surgeon Alan Gaynor claims that the search for beauty informs not only cultural history from antiquity forward, but the history of literature and philosophy as well. He finds that the "desire to be more beautiful, to look one's best, is as ancient as the human race," surveying practices from Egyptian and Greco-Roman antiquity (21). That desire remains universal, materializing with every glimpse into the mirror; as Richard Marfuggi proposes, "[J]ust about everyone on this planet looks into the mirror and sees *one* thing that they would change about themselves if they could" (4). Universal desire for physical beauty becomes complicit with philosophical and poetic aesthetics in Benjamin Gelfant's advocacy, which connects the importance of aesthetic surgery with the views of Percy Shelley, Bertrand Russell, George Santayana, and William Carlos Williams, who, taken together, are invoked to support the "fact" that beautiful people are "pleasing to the senses" (10). Statements from these canonical figures join the lesson we are taught by nature, that the "forces of attractiveness and revulsion" are "biologic," rather than social constructions (which, as many feminists argue, enslave us). For Gaynor and Gelfant, beauty is a desire that is unambiguous and prized, featured in terms of high sentiments and philosophic proof or scientific fact. Acknowledging the natural desire for natural beauty on a cosmological scale, patient and advocate Susan Gail puts prospective beautifiers into dialogue with cosmological intelligences, so that the questions of why and how to beautify come to occupy the mind of the universe: "I understand and respect the fact that the idea of talking to your universe may be a foreign concept for some people. If so, just do what it takes to relax yourself and seek guidance [about what modifications you need] from whatever power you chose [*sic*]. Be it God, Goddess, [or] Higher Power . . ." (23). Such elevation extends to imputations of the heroism of the aesthetic surgery patient, whom Jean Loftus associates with an epic struggle "to wage war against gravity, age, or genetics so that you may look and feel your best" (xx).

Alan Engler directs his apologia primarily at women with a chapter titled, "If They're Pretty, You Know They're Smart," which, as a way of recommending surgical beautifying, argues that children presume attractive teachers to be more intelligent than unattractive ones. This bias is not culturally conditioned, he argues, explaining, "In a startling demonstration of how early these prejudices appear, one-year-old children (who typically withdraw from strangers) withdrew more from the plain faces than from the attractive ones. Even three-month-old babies spent more time staring at pictures of attractive faces than at less attractive ones" (5). Like Gelfant, Engler acknowledges that the quest for beauty is "controversial," but resolves that controversy in the same way, by declaring that "beauty is an advantage throughout the animal kingdom" (4). Where Gelfant appeals to "normality," Engler appeals to "looking as good as one reasonably can" (9). These statements evade the complexity of what counts as being either "normal" or "reasonably" good looking, but have persuasive force to the extent that they use powerful concept terms. Sarnoff and Swirsky, too, introduce their guide to laser surgery by saying that the whole animal kingdom values beauty, and, in an effort to be inclusive, add that "people of all cultures and ethnic backgrounds endow physical attractiveness with the highest value" (15). All questioning of the social construction of beauty set aside, they simply cite, approvingly, the common perception that pretty girls are "good girls" (160). That analogy, between looking good and being good, is collapsed in the plain maxim so often given as a reason for aesthetic surgery: "to look and feel your best" (e.g., Loftus 2), which, as we will see further, represents the association of a beautified body with a healthy mind and a pure soul.

As Gelfant's acknowledgment of controversy over aesthetic surgery indicates, political implications do not go altogether unacknowledged by industry advocacies. Gelfant even mentions feminist critics such as Naomi Wolf and Nancy Friday in passing, but does so only to stress how interested all sorts of persons are in the subject of beauty. In general, beauty is featured as a centuries-old, apolitical pursuit, unrelated to cultural, racial, or gendered hegemony. Ideological implications are raised for barely a moment, and either dismissed or converted to a scientific argument. Thus, political issues are either overwhelmed or emptied out through recourse to an alternate set of topoi. Gelfant does this by referring to "biologic" beauty forces, and Gaynor's chapter titled "When Vanity Is Not A Sin" cites research associating the growing importance of physical attractiveness with increased geographic mobility and social fragmentation:

> I suspect that the growth in importance of physical attractiveness in today's society is partly due to our increased geographic mobility, as well as the concentration of our population in large urban areas. Because of these factors, people are now meeting more people in casual encounters than ever before. For example, it is estimated that the average twenty-year-old entering the job market will change jobs at least seven times during their working years. The divorce rate has risen over 700 percent since the turn of the century. In a society in which one cannot even count on having the same set of parents in our childhood for any length of time, the same marriage partner for any length of time; when one may be thrown in to the dating and mating market at age thirty, forty, fifty, sixty; when it becomes increasingly unlikely that one will have the same work-mates, colleagues, or neighbors for any length of time—in sum, in a society in which social fragmentation has proceeded to an unprecedented point, people are constantly assessed very quickly by others simply on the basis of their appearance rather than upon their record of actual behavior and other characteristics. Is it any wonder, then, that to help them cope, people look to the new keepers of the fountain of beauty and youth—the cosmetic surgeons, the dentists, the nutritionists, the cosmeticians, the physical therapists, and so on? (20)

While aesthetic surgery is featured as apolitical to the extent that it is responding to human nature in general, it is also a means of increasing one's power and influence in the polis (through more successful relationships and better jobs). Within this latter purpose there is an implicit argument describing less inequity in a society that makes beauty easy and accessible. In sum, the aesthetic surgical industry proposes that we are all in need of beau-tification to a greater or lesser extent, and presses us toward a condition that both fulfills a natural human desire and improves society through a good showing of bodies of its members.

CHAPTER 3

Outside-In

Abjection is at once a psychological, emotional, and physical phenomenon, which—in the case of, say, my repulsion at the sagging, wrinkled skin on my face and neck—involves the tension between the reality of an unruly semiotic (body) and the desire for an orderly symbolic (mind), along with the interanimation of reality and desire that keep the semiotic and symbolic, body and mind, inseparable. Objectifying the unruly semiotic and subjecting it to the symbolic enacts the desire for consubstantiality of body and mind, the desire to subject the body to the imaginary that the mind creates and maintains. Therefore, the process of objectification, abjection, and identification that informs a makeover culture governed by the aesthetic surgical imaginary necessarily involves an accommodation of the body to the mind, and to the Western superintendent of the mind, the soul. This accommodation is both a central issue in the history of Western philosophy and part of a strategic appeal by the makeover industries, including most prominently aesthetic surgery.

The historical and cultural process that prompted the growth of the aesthetic surgical industry—namely, the supplanting of an older moral and religious authority that viewed physical appearance as an extension of a moral condition by business enterprises that have begun to absorb medicine—has prompted an industry discourse fraught with repressions and ambivalences about the relationship of the body to the person's inner self. Historically, conceptions of the inner and outer selves have preserved a hierarchy that favors the inner self; the aesthetic surgical industry holds to this longstanding dualism, in which the inner self is primary and higher, the body a recalcitrant aspect that must be controlled.

The industry features its aesthetic administrations as a way of revaluing the body, disputing those who attribute vanity and superficiality to aesthetic surgical patients, and urging that the body be given the importance that it warrants. However, this valorizing of the body is only an apparent disruption of the inner/outer hierarchy, for two reasons: (1) the industry values only the body that defies its mutable nature, and accords with received beauty ideals; and (2) the industry ultimately engages a spiritualized rhetoric of renewal that functions both to elevate its attention to what is actually common—in this case, the ordinary states of bodily differing—to suggest that its work is of the highest import and to hold its practice above social politics. If the industry can succeed in featuring itself as an apolitical enterprise (thus not contributing to social discrimination and the pain of physically abjected groups) which is supported by the very heavens (one need not question the needs of the spirit, though one can always question the emotions), it lifts its ministrations beyond reproach, and hails patients with no less than the good and the true. Though it calls for a revaluation of the skin we live in, altering perceptions about aging and physical difference is not an industry concern; rather, it aims to rehabilitate the body to reflect the happiness and goodness of an inner self that transcends materiality and purifies the psyche.

The idea that the body can obstruct a beautiful inner self materializes in advertisements for restoring an outward appearance that reflects the real "you" inside. One typical ad urges consumers to "Rediscover The Beauty In Your Eyes," positing an originary but faded beauty that is never lost forever, but can reemerge when the skin around the eyes is improved. The beautiful inner self must be allowed to speak through the body rather than go mute from the ugliness of aging. Advertisements for facial procedures note that an unbeautified face can give a false impression of the inner self; those who suffer from drooping brows, for instance, sport "horizontal lines and furrows that can make a person appear angry, sad, or tired" (*Forehead Lift*). In answer, aesthetic surgeons claim to make the outside a vision of a positive inner state. Another ad declares that "Beauty is only skin deep," playing upon the familiar adage that beauty, and its associated goodness, is located both in and through the body, both on the surface and below or beyond it. Rather than denying beauty's depth, which would risk trivializing its importance, this ad affirms that the aestheticized skin reveals that depth. Another ad asks, "How would it be to have the wisdom of years and the face of youth?," creating a somatopsychic syllogism that premises the renewal of youth as the activity of wisdom and urges the conclusion that renovating the body is wiser than allowing for the appearance of aging that is traditionally associated with wisdom.[1]

The concept of a higher inner self is fundamental to an industry that features the individual, rather than society or culture, as the unit of positive change, and tied up with the industry's development of a spiritualized rhetoric of physical renewal. Surgeon Alan Gaynor argues that aesthetic surgery is not just "a practical and necessary adjunct to life, but far more importantly, [a practice that] . . . resonates from some of the deepest, most important and even spiritual parts of us" (17). Likewise, surgeon Alan Engler declares that when "the gap between body and state of mind is bridged by plastic surgery . . . Patients' spirits are uplifted along with their bodies" (32). Describing the power of the surgeon who alters the body to effect at once mental health and a sort of spiritual revival,[2] Engler represents the industry suggestion that fixing the body brings about the harmony of body, mind, and soul, so that aesthetic surgery becomes an activity invested not only with physical and psychological resonances, but also spiritual ones.

Alongside their injunction to fix the facial flaws that cause "emotional hurting," Ganny and Collini print a quotation attributed to Jean Cocteau:

> A flaw of the spirit
> Cannot be hidden on a face
> But a flaw of a face
> If one fixes it,
> Can put a spirit right. (127)

The alignment of the somatopsychic observation with a somatospiritual proposition reveals the core conception maintained by the aesthetic surgical imaginary, of a relationship between mind and body much like that articulated in Plato's *Phaedrus*, where the body appears to be an obstacle to the manifest virtue of the inner self. Developing its own neo-Platonic formula, the industry relies on a tripartite model of the individual, positing a susceptible mind (the psyche subject to anxiety over a bad appearance), an amendable body, and an essential self. The essential self is not always explicitly or alertly distinguished from mind, but does emerge as an isolable entity in statements by industry advocates such as Henry and Heckaman, who say, "Remember, changing your outer appearance will not change who you are inside. . . . It may, however, result in greater self-confidence and a sense of security about yourself . . ." (2–3).[3] Industry bibliographer and historian Mario Gonzalez-Ulloa discusses what we might call the outside-in benefit of aesthetic surgical intervention by invoking all three elements of being:

We have always known that inner psychic and spiritual changes bring about a new external radiance, but we are now discovering that the process also works in reverse: Change the external appearance—restore the lost years—of a person struggling continually against indifferent or negative social reactions, and the inner light that has died begins to glow once more. (81)[4]

The essential self, Gonzalez-Ulloa's "inner light," oftentimes corresponds to character, other times to what Western religion calls the soul.

Industry advocates sometimes suggest that emphasis on the importance of looking good does constitute a sort of body reclamation project in the face of a philosophical and religious history that stresses renunciation of the body. The industry's repositioning of the body's importance to selfhood recalls the Dantean Heaven in which redeemed souls nonetheless feel incomplete without their earthly bodies (*Paradiso* 14.40–66). Escape from the body into the eternal self and transcendent mind is given voice by Plato, elaborated and refined within early Christian thought, and tied to the physical facts of mortality that are related not only to illness and disease, but also to a dangerous sexuality that requires rigid surveillance and restraint. As Jean-Pierre Vernant proposes, the pre-Socratic, Homeric body was often that of the demigod, in whom the division between material and spirit, human and divine, is never clear. The god has superior powers of perception and strength and a home in the inaccessible beyond, but can also be embodied and interactive with the human world. In line with this presentation of the pre-Socratic body as irreducible to matter, Nicole Loraux observes that before the rise of Platonic thought, persons were thought to have a body (soma), and a *psuche*, which was not the same as a soul, but was liberated by death in the form of immortal glory. *Psuche* takes on the meaning of individual immortality with Plato's Socrates, who, as he dies, defines the philosopher as one who rejects the pleasures of the body so that his life resembles the existence of one whose only life is in the *psuche*.

If Platonic thought did not rigorously suppress the body (Socrates is both suspicious of the flesh and himself carnal), Christian neo-Platonism did. Peter Brown describes Roman and Greek culture that for the most part viewed procreation as the only way to approximate the transcendence of mortality, until Christianity began to focus on "a mortal body [that] weighed down the soul" (47), initiating a perceived antithesis between the flesh and the spirit that remains a fundament of Christianity today. Brown notes that Christianity abandoned the terms "body" and "soul," preferring "flesh," which implied weakness and temptation, and "spirit," which indicated a life utterly beyond connections with the body (47–49).[5] Kristeva, reviewing the rules of body waste avoidance and ritual procedures for purification of the menstruating woman in biblical Leviticus, stresses that the clean and proper body was formerly delineated by the religious state: "An unshakeable adherence to Prohibition and Law is necessary if that perverse interspace of abjection is to be hemmed in and thrust aside. Religion. Morality. Law" (*Powers* 16). The aesthetic surgical industry, of course, administers to the body's signs of corruption and difference, while it focuses on the repression of the abject woman and mother by largely directing its appeals to women's perceptions of physical inadequacy and rejection by the symbolic of beauty; thus, it is not surprising that Martha Reineke, who adapts Kristevan abjection to a study of medieval female mystics, sees the policing of the abject body—formerly the job of religion—as a primary activity of a contemporary medicine that has taken up the "sentry duty" of safeguarding "the borders that separate order from disorder, dispensing information, protection, and judgments" (246).[6] In the context of a spiritualized medicine, the operation of objectification, abjection, and identification includes, for each category, transcendence as a referent: One objectifies those body parts that contradict the presumed eternity of the inner self, and abjects them in order to eliminate the division between outer self and inner self, to identify with the incorruptible Law of the Father. The reconciliation of inner and outer selves thus enacts deference to a Symbolic that has defined the corrupt body as sinful and unqualified for paradise.

As Foucault proposes, by the third century the control of the self was not directed toward forming a healthy body, but toward superintending a body that is disorderly, fragile, and potentially damaging to the soul (*History of Sexuality*). The importance of a well-maintained body to a "life that is worthwhile and free of inconvenience" (Athanaeus in Foucault 101) legitimates advice on the care of the self early in the history of medicine:

> The increased medical involvement in the cultivation of the self appears to have been expressed through a particular and intense form of attention to the body. . . . The body the adult has to care for, when he is concerned about himself, is no longer the young body that needed shaping by gymnastics; it is a fragile, threatened body, undermined by petty miseries—a body that in turn threatens the soul, less by its too-vigorous requirements than by its own weaknesses. (56–57)

The "rapprochement (practical and theoretical) between medicine and ethics" (Foucault 57) leads to greater alertness to the imperfections of the body insofar as such alertness involves one constantly in the process of correction and improvement, and results in detection through the body of "diseases of the soul" which may otherwise "pass unnoticed" (Foucault 58).[7] The Plotinian thought that influences Christian asceticism leads eventually to an Augustinian insensibility to the body, and an insistence upon its renunciation (see, for example, Alliez and Feher; Tazi; Brown). But at all points in these developments, the soul cannot be absolutely dissociated from the body, so that "goodness" is manifest in appearance—beautiful, gluttonous, ascetic, diseased, aged, and so forth—and, mutatis mutandis, "looking good" coincides with both "feeling good" and "being good."

For both Caroline Walker Bynum and Nadia Tazi, recuperation of the body emerges in the Middle Ages as a kind of religious obsession with debating the nature of the corporeal self, rooted in "the fear of losing an identity that one feels is connected to the body" (Tazi 540). For Bynum, medieval speculation about "the resurrection of Christ's foreskin, about the 'teletransportation' of glorified bodies, or about the fate of eaten embryos," finds its contemporary counterpart in today's popular assumption that "in some way the body is the self" (249). This contemporary attitude not only continues medieval fascinations, but also reaches back to the sophistic conception of the soul as the source of bodily motion, a conception that is never wholly divorced from the "idea of grace as an effect produced by a graceful body" (Alliez and Feher 53). Thus, the aesthetic surgical industry derives a moral philosophy of medical purpose from the Western history of the body as well as an obsession with physical imperfection that maintains the body as the potential agent of good and appeals to the longstanding and paradoxical desire to both transcend and retain the body, to both elevate and lay claim to the full materiality of the self.[8]

For Barbara Stafford, the Enlightenment modernism that supplanted cosmological and religious epistemologies was driven by a desire to have exact knowledge of inexact things, and the body was one of the inexact things that science sought to diagnose. Thus the body's hidden parts and the mind's hidden character were to be discovered through anatomical dissection, microscopy, and phrenological and physiognomic practices. We think of this period as a time of intense empiricism, when natural and medical scientists probed the body and the physical world in order to understand, in full and concrete ways, physical and natural laws; however, Stafford's study suggests that the Enlightenment fascination with the body only served to drive interest back out into an abstract realm of the spirit and to cause researchers to come more forcefully to the conclusion that the body does not evidence its own truth and vitality, but is only a trace, or indicator, of loftier, more dependable truths.[9] Dominant philosophical and scientific traditions may be seen to resonate, then, with aesthetic surgeon Alan Engler's declaration that "[p]atients' spirits are uplifted along with their [aesthetically improved] bodies."

This position, which reflects that of the industry as a whole, proposes not only that aesthetic surgery merges outer and inner, but more importantly, that a prioritizing of inner self entails nomination of the body as primary emblem of its goodness. Though the aesthetic surgical industry does not speak explicitly of unimproved bodies as the housing of corrupt inner selves, it nonetheless reminds us of the well-rehearsed coincidence of monstrous looks with deranged mental states. This association, one that perhaps most famously occupies Mary Shelley's *Frankenstein*, continues as a staple of the modern horror genres. *Mr. Sardonicus*, a horror film released in 1961, is a notable entry into the bodily imaginary of the first decade of the "New Age," which saw a surge in approval for cosmetic surgery developing in tandem with an urgent interest in techniques for self-improvement that centralized the importance of self-image, and the strengthening cultural belief that we ought not let ourselves go toward a bad appearance (Haiken 155). Exploring the power of the outside-in relationship as a complex dialectic among psychological and physiological sources of pathology, the film articulates the coincidence of a corrupt body and an unhappy mind, but leaves uncertain which, the body or the mind, is the first cause of a corrupt inner self.

Baron Sardonicus is a wicked man with a deformed face. But he was once Marek, a good and good-looking man, intent upon pleasing a wife who wanted wealth and glamour beyond what their simple farm life could provide. Marek's father buys his son and daughter-in-law a lottery ticket and dies soon after, the winning ticket buried with him in his vest. Upon learning that the lottery ticket was a winner, Marek's wife insists that Marek invade his father's grave to retrieve the ticket. He does, and emerges with his face frozen into the same death mask as his father's, locked in a mordant grimace. He becomes "Baron Sardonicus," using his lottery winnings to establish himself as a reclusive nobleman whose grotesque face is always masked and who pursues a horrible career of torturing, raping, and murdering village women whom he lures to his estate, while he desperately seeks a therapy that can save him. Sardonicus's horrifying visage is the manifestation of what he terms "shock and guilt" at his own ghoulish act, and he believes that his bad looks have made him bad inside. Life in a corrupt body has, he says, "erased all decency and human feeling from my heart." He summons an eminent English physician, Sir Robert Cargrave, famous for his successes at reversing paralysis, and tells the doctor that, "[i]t is for [him] to restore" not just Sardonicus's face, but also his inner goodness. Sardonicus believes that his soul will be healed when he is good-looking again; tortured by the belief that he is evil, he calls for a facelift. However, Cargrave does not believe that Sardonicus needs aesthetic surgery; rather, he thinks that Sardonicus's death mask, because a symptom of his shock and guilt at abusing his father's corpse, will lift once Sardonicus is made to relive his trauma. This dispute over the proper treatment for the ailing Sardonicus does not resolve the question, however, whether ugliness makes one criminal, or crime makes one ugly. In either case, beauty and goodness are meaningfully linked, though in the first case, aesthetic surgery can be a cure for a man gone bad, and in the second, psychotherapy is called upon to transform the body.

Henry's and Heckaman's revaluing of the body echoes Sardonicus's belief in the coincidence of good appearance and good character:

> Vanity was believed by the Greeks to be a sister of Beauty and Justice and a virtue. What happened? Beauty was knocked from her pedestal by the sword of a well intentioned but now outworn puritanical notion that attention paid to the body took something away from the soul. These principles are not mutually exclusive. (199)

The advocacy of body obsession as kin to established virtues, like justice, rings with a paradox that is embedded in the antique and neo-Platonic traditions it invokes: in the *Phaedo*, Socrates' arguments for the primacy of philosophic truth are interspersed with his deliberate interest in his own body, whose gradual deadening he observes so explicitly and carefully, not at all indifferent, making the body central to a discourse devoted to escaping it (Loraux 34–39). Offering a resolution of this paradox, through its harmonizing of body, psyche, and spirit, the aesthetic surgical industry implies that those who do not beautify are choosing a pitiable asceticism over the good life of the good body: they are, in the words of surgeon Ronald Levine, "granola heads" (Toughill A17). On the other hand, those who associate beauty, virtue, wisdom, and good looks (and who have the means to maintain those associations) are offered the prospect of bodies that reflect the quality of their souls.

The body out of harmony with psyche and spirit is the abject body of the monster, who is deadly and, in religious terms, satanic. While monsters such as Frankenstein's Creature and Baron Sardonicus frame a tradition of corrupt, ravaging males, it is the female body that remains most susceptible to corruption, most distant from achieving the transcendent intellect that the Western philosophical tradition aligns with the eternal soul (see, for example, Agonito; Covino). The Medusa, the Witch, and their materializations in the "loathly lady" literary tradition most prominently figured by Chaucer and Spenser comprise a typology of horrific female bodies who are figures of eternal evil and staples of popular culture. At the same time that such figures have been adapted as countercultural sources of defiant feminist power, as deities of the "monstrous feminine," they remain the abjects of a mass culture subtended by the aesthetic surgical imaginary, as we see in, for instance, the *Alien* series of horror movies that continued through the 1970s, 1980s, and 1990s. Barbara Creed locates signs of the abject mother/monster at a number of points in the lair where the murderous creatures live in *Alien 2*, "in the images of birth, the representations of the primal scene, the womblike imagery, the long winding tunnels leading to inner chambers, the rows of hatching eggs" (19). Ripley, the heroic "good" mother, represents the slide between the semiotic mother and the symbolic order when she both cares for the orphan Newt and wields masculine power over the monstrous archaic mother. In *Alien 2*, she appears, despite her kindly maternal function relative to Newt, as a hyperorderly, technologized fighting machine, encased by a futuristic loading vehicle that serves both as armor and weaponry against the attacking alien mother, and transforms Ripley herself into a monstrous defense against the monster. Given that abjection is not just a paranoid projection of the paternal order, but a fearful reality of the body's primitive past and future condition, we could see Ripley as a heroine rightly called upon to protect the survival of the human species. On the other hand, because the *Alien* movies capitalize on archaic-mother embodiments of abjection, we also see cyborg Ripley as drawn into the paternal fantasy of the abject mother, as the Holy Virgin's alter image, a woman called upon to represent the interests of the Paternal Order as the embodiment of one of its computer-driven vehicles of commerce. Fused with the technological imaginary, Ripley fights so that Newt's "outside," all innocence and child beauty, is not invaded by the ravaging abject mother, who inserts her eggs inside living human bodies, where they gestate and eventually explode through the body-womb. Ripley the technomother succeeds in preserving for Newt the consubstantiality of outside and inside.

Significantly, the monstrous abject mother is not deranged as the result of a division between the corrupt body and the virtuous self/soul (as in the prototypical *Dr. Jekyll and Mr. Hyde*). She is unclean, and thus deranged by nature, a figure of corruption from puberty forward, when her menstruating body begins to perform her defilement. The cultural maintenance of the abject mother/monster makes the desire to identify with the transcendent body that much more urgent for women and helps to explain why the focus of the aesthetic surgical imaginary on female patients is so effective. Embedded in and inculcated by a hegemonic religious and philosophical tradition that has satanized the body that is not sanitized, we objectify those features or parts that vary from the transcendent body as elements of both physical and moral corruption approaching the monstrous. Ironically, the urgency for a consubstantial inside and outside that conform to the cultural presentation of integrity and virtue is often voiced as the denial of cultural influence; as we will see in chapter 4, the insistence by aesthetic surgical patients that "I'm doing it for me" ostensibly isolates desire from the imaginary that interpellates it, while also voicing a cliché of the institutional lexicon that surrounds and drives the patient's choices. In other words, the declaration of individualism and self-will is part of the script that the governing imaginary has written.

CHAPTER 4

"I'm Doing It for Me"

The transformation of abject realities into tidy materializations of conventional, individualistic, bourgeois desire and belief finds a willing medium in turn-of-the-century television, which, while it has always been absorbed with the packaging of reality,[1] turns increasingly to "reality" shows during the first part of this century, in which the camera watches nonactors living out parts of their lives. The televised reality of the aesthetic surgical imaginary occupied its first regular time slot on October 25, 2001, with the debut on cable television's Learning Channel of *A Personal Story*. This thirty-minute program, which continues to air every weekday at this writing, primarily presents women who, because they are discontent with their bodies, elect to have aesthetic surgery. From a Kristevan perspective, we observe that each story is about the desire to defeat or overcome abjection. Though each episode is about the aspiration to bring the body under control and within conventional beauty norms, the program masks the cultural determination of the personal, and sidesteps the question of desires generated outside the "self." In other words, although each patient is enacting the process of objectification, abjection, and identification, the cultural ideology that directs this process is both denied (by the patient) and disguised (by the production). To explicate this proposition, I will describe some of the I-centered narratives that comprise the typical *Personal Story*, during which a prospective patient moves from dissatisfaction with the body, to consultation, to surgery, to a newfound satisfaction with the body, and indicate the ways in which the patient's repeated declarations that self-image is purely a matter of personal feeling and choice ("I'm doing it for me") are located in a culturally determined sense of what is "best" for the body. By insistently separating the personal from the cultural, *A Personal Story* delivers the aesthetic surgical industry from responsibility for its patients' desires and does not let us see that such cultural institutions set the parameters of abjection and its remedies.

The Learning Channel (TLC) is a subsidiary of Discovery Communications, whose Discovery channel first aired in 1985, with approximately 156,000 U.S. subscribers,[2] and had grown by 2002 well beyond live coverage of world news events, support of educational initiatives, and enhancement of school readiness, into retail sales, online programming, and production of home and leisure programs. With a strong international presence, the Discovery Channel in 2002 had more than 650 million subscribers in 155 countries and territories worldwide. As its website claims, "Few media companies have the distribution, impressions and cross platform capability that Discovery has around the world" (August 24, 2002).[3]

TLC, in particular, which first appeared in 1991 and began as a network aimed primarily at enhancing school readiness for children, was distributed in 2002 to more than 87 million homes, and has developed a programming approach that expands the sources of learning well beyond the classroom, pursuing a prevailing sense that information—of all sorts—*is* education. *Ready, Set, Learn!*, TLC's original offering for preschoolers, remains on its schedule; the rest has been radically transformed:

> Ranked as one of cable television's top 20 networks,[4] TLC's programming runs the gamut from medical to modern marvels and dating to babies. On weeknights, TLC features some of cable television's most successful series, including the breakout hit *Junkyard Wars* and the Emmy Award-winning *Trauma: Life in the ER*. TLC's original daytime series, including *A Wedding Story* and *A Baby Story* are among the top-rated daytime series among women 18–34. Redefining the idea of "how-to," TLC launched the series Trading Spaces, where friends and neighbors swap houses to redecorate a room. (http://tlc.discovery.com, August 24, 2002)

The TLC web page invites the prospective surgical patient to have her or his "personal story told on national television":

> A Personal Story is a heart-warming 30-minute TLC program featuring real people undergoing re-constructive and elective cosmetic surgery. Each show will document the patient's personal experience as they approach and undergo surgery and how the outcome impacts the quality

of their life. We are looking for stories about adults, teens, children and even babies. Family and friends and the surgeon must be available for videotaping.

Patients or parents who want to apply must obtain permission from their surgeons prior to filling out the application. Doctors who would like to recommend patients must have the approval of the patient before sending in the application.

Applicants must be at least 18 years old. If the patient is under 18 years of age, we must have full parental approval, supervision and participation in the videotaping. All applicants/patients must be comfortable sharing their surgery story with our national audience.

Because this is a documentary production there is no compensation paid to the patients or the doctors featured. (http://www.apersonalstory.com/glines.html, August 24, 2002)

The TLC claim that it presents "life unscripted" (http://tlc.discovery.com, August 24, 2002) contributes to the ethos of the natural that generally informs the aesthetic surgical imaginary, and the emphasis on patient decisions as wholly self-willed, while it supports a value-neutral conception of the presentation, as one free of commercial, corporate, or institutional motives. Attention to the ways in which *A Personal Story* is indeed scripted reveals a complex effort to render a clean and proper story, an effort which reflects the larger cultural consciousness invoked and legitimated by the aesthetic surgical imaginary. As we have already noted, the aesthetic surgical industry rejects the suggestion that it is in any way part of the problem of abject body image; rather, it sees itself as contributing to a solution to this problem (that is, benevolence is at the heart of its administrations). In this connection, featured patients on *A Personal Story* often remark that no one is pressuring them into having surgery to improve appearance; instead, friends and family, though supportive of the surgical decision, claim that surgery is unnecessary, and that they love and accept the prospective patient just the way she is. In sum, every patient who tells *A Personal Story* is presented as self-determined, part of a caring context, and emotionally healthy—apart from a basic dissatisfaction with the body that causes common feelings of self-consciousness and low self esteem—and thus perfectly able to make this particular decision.

Each episode of *A Personal Story* follows a formula for presentation in which we see the featured patient at four stages of her (very occasionally his) surgical process, that I would describe as (1) Testimony, (2) Consultation, (3) Surgery, and (4) the Afterlife. Featured patients begin by introducing the viewer to family, friends, children, even pets, oftentimes in the home setting, occasionally somewhere in the outdoors. The patient testifies to the body problem she would like to fix: the origins of and her past struggles with the unsatisfactory area of the body; the centrality of a good body image to her life (she will often say that her physical appearance is inconsistent with the person she feels herself to be, or would like to be); and the presence of the full approval and support of others (even though others do not necessarily believe that she needs the surgery). She relates her hopes and expectations concerning the surgery's outcome, and finally, reaffirms her decision to proceed.

During the Consultation segment, we meet the physician who will perform the surgery; he or she makes comments, which can be general (patients need to have appropriate expectations), or specific to the patient (she's going to get this kind of result, feel better, and so on.) The surgeon often provides drawings to illustrate the surgical process and show how the body will be altered. The patient declares her faith in the chosen surgeon, speaking of the surgeon's good reputation, or, occasionally, revealing that she is actually employed in the surgeon's practice. This is often followed by a reaffirmation of the patient's decision to have surgery. Patients with children are often seen making preparations for the care of the children during the surgical process and recovery period.

The Surgery segment often presents the patient checking into the surgical facility and being rolled into the operating room. The patient then undergoes the procedure while the surgeon explains the process to viewers while performing it, oftentimes featuring the names and functions of the surgical tools, and sometimes discussing the surgeon's operative preferences:

> I do this procedure [breast enlargement] with the arms tucked at the side, because I do a sub-muscular approach. With the arms tucked at the side, it relaxes this muscle, and I find that as the implant expands, it gives me a better idea of what I'm gonna get. If the arms are out, this muscle, the pectoralis major muscle, tightens up. I used to do it with the arms out, and I just find that I get a better post-operative result in the long term, because I get a better idea of what pocket I'm dealing with at the time of surgery. (May 16, 2002)

Despite the specificity of this surgeon's description, what I would call "the abjection factor" is carefully controlled throughout the surgery. The viewer does glimpse unpleasant things, such as fat passing through tubes and big "steaks" of cut-away flesh going into measuring containers, but she does not see flesh being sliced, organs revealed where skin, tissue, and muscle have been excised, or stitches reconnecting areolas to breast areas. As liposuction canulas are seen to pummel areas of the body, the focus is much more on the surgeon's skillful motions than on the body being pummeled. In such cases, the visuals function to feature the excised parts of the body as the ugly, alien enemy, and to suppress the hurt being done to the body as a sensate entity. Following surgery, we see the surgeon checking in with the patient's family or friends, assuring them that the surgery has gone well. We then see the patient pn the gurney awake but groggy. This segment often ends with surgeons affirming the importance of their work.

Finally, in the Afterlife segment, which takes places from three to ten weeks following surgery, the patient will often comment on her experience, including the pain she has endured during the recovery period, though not more than a few seconds is spent on this. (Occasionally, the surgeon will also comment on the recovery.) The patient quickly moves to discussion of her happiness with the results, reaffirming her decision to have the surgery through the modeling of new clothes, and the testimony of mates, family, and friends, who are delighted by the patient's changed body and sense of selfhood. Before and After pictures are displayed. Each episode of *A Personal Story* ends with patients celebrating their outcomes, declaring that the surgery has given them an utterly new lease on life, motivating them to, for instance, go back to school, or dance in public.

There are no mistaken desires, no bad outcomes on *A Personal Story*. The show's website, in fact, tells us that final segments of the show "will be one full day with the patient and their family and friends for a follow-up on how wonderful things have turned out" (October 20, 2002). The duplication in each thirty-minute segment of a standard, easily digested plot sequence indicates that the show functions not to educate the viewer about aesthetic surgical processes, as we might expect from the "Learning Channel," but rather to normalize, routinize, and legitimate the industry as a response to the personal desires of individuals.[5]

The emphasis on life-altering impact coincides with the implication that the changes *Personal Story* patients undergo are permanent, and in that regard, the program reinforces the industry proposition that the body can receive the blessing of deep and lasting therapeutic change.[6] This ostensible permanence accounts for the increasing popularity of the term "aesthetic"—rather than the term "cosmetic"—for describing procedures that improve appearance. "Aesthetic surgery" is a more recent and less familiar term than "cosmetic surgery," though the former has been in official use for nearly half a century. The first congress of the International Confederation of Plastic, Reconstructive, and Aesthetic Surgery convened in 1955, and the American

Society for Aesthetic Plastic Surgery was founded in 1967 (the older and more influential American Society of Plastic and Reconstructive Surgery was founded in 1931). Sander Gilman's focus in his scholarly work on aesthetic surgery results in part from his awareness that all attempts to alter body appearance are tied to cultural and racial conceptions of beauty. Further, he recognizes that the medical profession attempts to dissociate cosmetic surgery from a pejorative identification with the beauty industry by maintaining "the idea of the 'beautiful' without using the terms beauty or cosmetic" (*Creating Beauty* 14).

Interested in how conceptions of beauty from antiquity forward have influenced our desires to "remake the self," and how those desires have been addressed by medicine, Gilman offers "aesthetic surgery" as a comprehensive term for naming a range of procedures variously called "plastic," "reconstructive," or "cosmetic." This term, which Gilman adopts in order to give critical scope and precision to his work, has become increasingly common in commercial use; in a proliferation of aesthetic surgery institutes or centers; in advertisements that picture classical artworks such as *the Mona Lisa* and Michelangelo's *David* in order to stress that "when choosing a plastic surgeon, an artistic touch means as much as great credentials;" in descriptions of remodeled aesthetic patients as "Classically Contoured"; and in the naming of beauty enhancement procedures to stress the shaping of the body into a new artistic object: Three Dimensional Liposculpture, Permanent Lip Enhancement, and Feathertouch Skin Resurfacing. While cosmetic products and procedures are increasingly associated with temporary remedies, aesthetic projects, accompanied often by the metaphor of sculpture, are distinctive for their long-lasting effects.

Emphasis on the aesthetic is clear in the first seconds of each *Personal Story* episode when we see a nicely proportioned and statuesque young woman in a leotard moving gracefully across the screen while the names of aesthetic procedures flash around and across her body, announcing the possibility that one's body can be refigured, in both the verbal and visual senses of that term, as a new aesthetic object. A list of terms entering from screen left meets a list entering from screen right, acting as dyads that suggest the new attitudes and self-image that follow from surgery: liposuction/self-esteem; reconstructive/confidence; eyelift/pride; breast augmentation/dignity. This sequence of industry terminology, written on the body of an idealized patient, ends with the program's title: *A Personal Story*; thus, the overall indication of this sequence is that the institutional lexicon and its illustration precede and define the personal, that the personal *is* the institutional.

Aesthetic surgery is a serious business—involving risk, pain, cutting, family concerns, the desire for self-improvement—calculated to meet the demand that social subjects care for and control the body, that they not deny themselves beauty, or passively give up control of their psychophysical selves. Persons who appear on the show surely experience this range of considerations and exigencies, and to some extent confirm reputable psychological and sociological work on body image as central to self-image, self-understanding, and social success.

As we have seen, "abjection" refers to the casting off of the unwanted other; in bodily terms, this is made up of the waste and fluids that suggest death, disorder, and the lack of clear boundaries. Kristeva is interested also, though not extensively, in abjection as a social phenomenon: how the woman and the racial other, for instance, come to be abjected in culture. The analogy between the social body and the individual body is one that occupies Kristeva, who recognizes that for both cases, the abject is constructed as the lower term of a binary, with the heterogeneity within a symbolic structure perceived as the "waste" of the system ("The System and the Speaking Subject" 31). Just as the body must abject its waste in order to survive (*Powers* 3), so does the symbolic identify and eliminate some of its own content in order to thrive, to know what it is (not). Thus, the abject is always being articulated (though negatively) by and within the systems that seek to dispel it. The fetishizing of wholeness and integration, then, is part of an imaginary that the body just does not abide or respect; the clean and proper body valorized by the social symbolic is a fantasy. Within the aesthetic surgical imaginary, rejuvenated and redefined flesh stands for an other, an abject, that can be contained, in both senses: present within and brought under control. The aesthetic surgical patient can be secure from, and thus a cut above, the suppressed or menacing conditions of mortality, benefiting from a binary construction of the body in which the good body must be estranged and literally separated from its abject counterpart. By featuring a narrative of personalized discontent, in which aspects of the body are said to be inconsistent with an inner sense of self, aesthetic medicine sidesteps questions of socially and culturally constructed abjection. But in reality, aesthetic medicine can really only help us by developing concepts of health and beauty that encourage the viability of living in tension with the variant body, of expanding our appreciation of "allowable" bodies; of allowing the unthinkable body to coexist with the body that we can and do think through culture.[7]

Each *Personal Story* is structured around an individual's articulation of her orientation toward her body. With this emphasis, it differs from other

2001–2002 medical docudramas that tend to focus on the medical institution and the physicians more than the patient, as their titles alone indicate: *Houston Medical, Trauma: Life in the ER;* [Johns] *Hopkins 24/7.* While all contemporary medical docudramas invite personal attention to the patients under treatment, *A Personal Story* sets itself apart by making the patient the exclusive voice-over narrator. This implicitly aligns the personal, and its associations with sincerity and authenticity, with the direct utterances of the speaking subject. This feature also serves to establish the psychological soundness of the patient, who is seen to speak for herself, rationally and decisively. In the course of each program, there are clips of the patient's friends and family and the physician, speaking to the camera, but no off-camera voice is heard prompting their responses. They are, then, like the patient, speaking "for themselves," apparently unmediated, and on topics raised in the patient's voice-over. So if this "supporting cast" is being directed at all, it appears to be directed by the patient herself, and cautioned to offer nothing but (1) praise for the patient's choice, and (2) assurances that they love her with or without the surgery, as with the little daughter of a woman about to undergo liposuction who, though just seven years old, concludes with a maturity that seems almost scripted; "If [my mother] wants to [have liposuction], then she can go right for it, but I don't think she really needs it because she looks fabulous already" (17 May 2002).

In her now classic essay, "Visual Pleasure and Narrative Cinema," Laura Mulvey tells us that three visual perspectives define film: the camera's record of the profilmic event, the looks at one another by characters within the film, and the viewing of the filmed event by the audience.[8] We are supposed to forget about the first two, so that we may be entirely caught up in the illusion of projecting ourselves onto the screen characters and into their looks at one another. Alternative, radical filmmakers, Mulvey proposes, begin by "free[ing] the look of the camera into its materiality in time and space and the look of the audience into dialectics and passionate detachment," so that the "pleasure and privilege . . . [of being] the 'invisible guest'" is smashed (448). Though Mulvey is interested primarily in how the gaze, or "looking relation" (Gaines), produced through narrative and camera techniques in film is voyeuristic and male, her theory can also be used to discuss the ostensibly unmediated viewpoint that *A Personal Story* presents to its audience, encouraging the audience to view the patient as a kind of free agent. The patient is both a real subject and an interpellated figure, yet the camera and narrative techniques used to generate the program remove the patient's body from association with the processes of its historical and cultural production.

Below I feature representative episodes of *A Personal Story* in order to discuss in some detail how various narrative and camera techniques function to hide or deny (or, in psychological terms, repress) the circumstances of cultural, historical, and economic production that are necessarily part of each program.[9] The point of such a discussion, acknowledging that all communication media are necessarily strategic and selective in their condensed representation of experience, is always worth making again, especially as the media claim to be representing unmediated reality becomes more widespread. But more important for our purposes here is the observation that abjection is the basis for a television show that is sponsored by its denial, and that the desire and consequence of abjection—identification with the hegemonic imaginary—is bracketed away through strategic scripting and editing that are complicit with the patient's expressed understanding of her actions as individualistic and self-willed.

"ANA'S ALOHA BODY"

Ana Alvarez wants a tummy tuck and a breast lift and enlargement to counteract the effects of time, gravity, and multiple childbirths. Her *Personal Story* presents a consultation with her surgeon, Grant Stevens, as if this event is exploratory and prior to both her election of a procedure and her choice of a surgeon. The segment is, however, fabricated, since an appearance on *A Personal Story* requires the application and formal commitment of both patient and surgeon prior to the episode's filming. Nonetheless, in the filmed consultation, Ana behaves as if she is uncertain about what to do.

At one point, she asks Dr. Stevens whether "this is the right thing I should be doing." Though we cannot determine the intentionality of Ana's question, the issue of "rightness" conceivably includes the ethical, aesthetic, psychological, economic, and cultural elements of her decision. However, Dr. Stevens confines his answer to discussion of Ana's physical features:

> [T]his is the perfect thing you should be doing here. You're a great candidate for this. You have minimal amounts of breast sagginess and abdominal fullness, but enough to justify surgery. We can do both procedures in a timely fashion, and the nice thing is that we're not increasing the risk, by combining them and doing them both together. (June 7, 2002)

It is noteworthy that Dr. Stevens has already spoken with Ana during the consultation about the clinical aspects of her case, having examined Ana's breasts and abdomen, and commented on the measurements and hang of her breasts, as well as on the extent of stretch mark removal that the abdominoplasty will accomplish. In this context, Ana's question seems artificial, positioned rhetorically for the purpose of featuring the industry as not unreceptive to questioning, even as the moment for genuine inquiry has clearly already passed. This is an ostensibly personal story and personal decision, yet the discourse is restricted to the clinical, ignoring the ethical, psychological, moral, and cultural implications of the decision.

In this regard, it is important to notice what has been left out of the personal as presented. Omitted from Ana's story, for instance, is any consideration of the cost of the surgery, which, since she appears to be the single mother of minor children, we might expect to be a significant issue. Costs are never explicitly discussed on *A Personal Story*, and Ana quite explicitly dissociates her surgery from acts of purchasing:

> I'm so pleased with my surgery that I just want to tell everybody that it is so worth it, absolutely worth it. How can you buy self-esteem? You can't. Self-esteem is priceless. And basically this is what it's about: if there's something that's gonna help you feel better about yourself, just do it.

Ana implies that there are costs to having surgery, but this seems unconnected to money. From other expressed worries about pain, scarring, and the surgical outcome, Ana suggests that the physical discomfort and emotional uncertainty connected with her aesthetic surgery constitute a kind of cost, yet her own statements about "being cut from one end of your hip to the other end of your hip" are thereupon destabilized by a string of affirmations:

> I was really determined that I was gonna heal myself as quickly as possible. It's been 4 weeks and 2 days, one month, since my surgery, and I feel fabulous! It just makes a world of a difference. I feel very, I feel great about how I look. . . . [Shown stretching on the beach with a friend, Ana continues.] It's funny because people go, "Gee Ana, you look like a bombshell now," you know. And I do feel sexier, you know, I do. . . . [Then, picking out bikinis, which Ana claims not to have done since the age of 19, she adds,] I'm happy. I'm so pleased. . . . It's fun to be youthful. It's fun to look good. It's fun to stay fit. Take a little time for yourself, you know, and make it fun.

Clearly, any recognition that surgery involves difficulty is quickly replaced by immediate assurances that all will turn out right in the end.

This is, of course, how capitalism interpellates its subjects: by concealing the processes of production, which include not only costs and payments, but also pain, scarring, and emotional anxiety. Finally, this *Personal Story* is an unqualified advertisement for an unquestionably desirable procedure, one whose rightness and costs are not marked by either ambivalence or ambiguity, even at the point that we watch Dr. Stevens draw the lines of incision on Ana's body with a black marker (as he prepares to permanently inscribe the marks of the aesthetic surgical imaginary), an act accompanied only by cheerful, quasi-mathematical talk about the prefigured outcome.

"Fatima's Flawless Nose"

Ana's episode begins to indicate how *A Personal Story* constructs a scripted and idealized version of aesthetic surgical reality. At the same time that *A Personal Story* skirts the difficulties of having surgery, or makes these difficulties part of a heroic narrative, it also presents the social world as a willing and supportive part of the patient's decision-making process. These are stories about togetherness, the togetherness of the featured patient with supportive and loving others. In one episode, Fatima Curley, a twenty-nine-year-old Denver, Colorado, woman of mixed race (her father is African American, her mother a German immigrant), tells the story of having her nose altered. During a voice-over in which Fatima describes herself and life in Denver, she is seen on a skating excursion with three of her friends. Each friend discusses her relationship with Fatima. Kathy Lee tells us, "Fatima is one of my best friends," great to talk with, great to travel with. Kathy says that Fatima has had a long-standing concern about her nose, and she identifies with Fatima's problem, since she (Kathy) has experienced an inverse dissatisfaction with her nose: "We would laugh because I would say that I wanted to get mine bigger, and she wanted to get hers smaller, and so we could say that we'd take some of her nose and put it on my nose, and we'd be the perfect pair" (June 10, 2002). Kari Gratz cites her shared experience with Fatima when the two were Denver Bronco cheerleaders and, with friend Tammy Matsuo, affirms Fatima's decision to have aesthetic surgery, even though Fatima does not, in her friends' approving eyes, "need it." Throughout this segment, the women are shown frolicking together on the ice in the outdoors, spinning, and laughing at one another's falls.

Following another scene in which Fatima's mother, Susie Curley, herself a rhinoplasty patient, tells us that Fatima was always such a beautiful person that she "always managed somehow to be in the spotlight," Fatima and her friends are shown shopping together. Fatima tells them the story of the first time she became aware that her nose was perceived by others as too big. Her mother then testifies that she, too, always had a big nose; Fatima's father, Joe, tells us that he was surprised to learn that Fatima was self-conscious. Fatima's parents sit in on her consultation with Dr. Brent J. Smith and discuss the recovery period with her following the appointment. Fatima is then shown speaking by phone with her brother, Tony, because he, too, underwent rhinoplasty. Finally, Fatima discusses this call with her parents just before she and they leaf through the family photo album, tracing the growth of Fatima's nose.

I cite this cheery and supportive context not in order to minimize the importance of family and friendship, but to point out homogeny in the narrative, which never portrays patients, before or after surgery, in a state of alienation. No scenes of waiting in cold medical offices, no sense that patients worry over expenses, no unsupportive mothers, fathers, or spouses. In a voiceover, Fatima speaks of her extensive support system: "My parents will be with me the very first day after the surgery. My girlfriend, Holly, had said she would take care of me for a couple of days. And also Kathy said she would help me. I don't know how I'll feel after that, if I can kind of take care of myself. So, friends and family will be there." When Fatima notes that her surgery will help her to become more outgoing, there is the suggestion that aesthetic surgery makes one more impervious to othering, and this feature is, of course, consistent with so much advertisement of aesthetic surgery that features its contributions to greater social and career success.

In the postsurgery segment, Fatima visits a spa with her friends and the group discusses Fatima's surgery and its results while they have their nails done, and later again during a trip to the gym. Nearly all scenes in *A Personal Story* are group scenes and all groups are, in effect, support groups. All interactions are optimistic and celebratory, consistent with the "Botox party," the current trend representing aesthetic surgery as an opportunity for social celebration. Growing in popularity through 2002, and most prevalent in the states with the highest aesthetic surgical patient populations (California, Florida, New York, Texas), the Botox party is a gathering of prospective patients at a house or apartment, where each is given injections of botulinum toxin to paralyze the muscles whose everyday use can cause facial lines. Guests sample cheese cubes and sip Chardonnay ("Now they call them Botox 'seminars'"), while watching each other go under the needle. On *A Personal Story*, we are presented with a kind of "surgery party," and even though the social group collected is always rather small, it nonetheless serves as an intersubjective validation of the patient's decision, often expressed in the cultural clichés of sovereign individualism: Tammy says of Fatima, "If she's excited, I'm excited for her." The group affirms the individual, whose decision affirms the aesthetic surgical industry. The decision to have surgery becomes the source of good times, with the implication that those who do not make this decision are not taking the occasion to revitalize a circle of love and attention.

Barbara Fletcher, featured in the episode "Dad's Nose Goes," joins her mother in a double-voiced explanation of the way in which Barbara's past experiences have informed her decision to decrease the size of her nose:

> Barbara: After I had my son Tyler, nine years ago, the day before I had him, I was 250 pounds. . . . [There were] a few years there where I completely changed as a person and was pretty unhappy.
>
> Martha Fletcher: She was depressed. She tended to depend on food as a comfort, and a situation that she was not happy in. She came home and she started putting her life back together and making a life for her and Tyler.
>
> Barbara: Me and my mom went on a diet, a low fat diet.
>
> Martha: I had been diagnosed with high cholesterol. Well, Barbara wanted to be supportive.
>
> Barbara: I just started getting real active, like riding, horseback riding, and trying to keep busy. It took me about a year. And I lost probably about 90 pounds. I felt real great when I got rid of those extra pounds.
>
> Martha: Barbara had totally evolved from a very dark place in her life, back into the light, and it's wonderful to see that we have our daughter back. She's still working on herself, and this procedure that she's getting ready to have is probably part of that. Part of that self-esteem and self-imaging that she's still going through . . .
>
> Barbara: It's been a long road, and it's been a tough road, and I just kind of had to look deep into myself to find out what made me happy. And I've thought about this procedure for quite some time. Part of it's self-esteem to help me. After all I've been through, I think it's something I deserve. (June 10, 2002 11:30 a.m.)

Barbara's weight loss made her deserving of affiliation and reconciliation following a difficult period of single motherhood and significant weight gain. A good candidate for aesthetic surgery, Barbara is in a state of self-separation, but is already well along on the path toward recentralization with self and others. The camera becomes part of this approval process, acting as another kind of friend for the featured guest. Even the music on *A Personal Story* often functions to portray an integrated scene. In Barbara's case, a happy bluegrass tune accompanies her into the surgical facility and greets her following surgery.

"Light in Jodi's Eyes"

Jodi Renée Lang holds two master's degrees—one in educational psychology with emphasis in gifted, talented, and creative education, and one in interdisciplinary consciousness studies with an emphasis in holistic health, transpersonal psychology, and Eastern philosophy. She has also just completed a PhD, an accomplishment that becomes a motivation, among others, for having aesthetic surgery:

> The recent changes in my life have been numerous in the last year and a half I would say. I've recently left a relationship of 17 years, I've just gone through a major illness and a surgery, I have just completed a Doctorate degree, my degree in East-West psychology which is very exciting for me to complete it. I looked in the mirror one morning and something didn't look right with my eyes. They looked droopy to me, and they seemed foreign to me, and there was a knowing that I had just gone through a lot of changes. (June 17, 2002, 11:00 a.m.)

Committed to not doing "anything to alter [her] face for vanity," Jodi now finds she needs "an external change" in order that her eyes correspond with "how she sees from an internal perspective." As Jodi says, "I'm basically a very light, and light-hearted, person, and my eyes aren't reflecting that right now."

In the episode featuring Jodi, both the pre- and postsurgical scenes identify aesthetic surgery as part of a spiritual symbolic. Jodi tells us

> Meditation's important to me because it's a form of me being present and aware. If I didn't meditate every day, I'm not so sure that I would be as balanced when obstacles were thrown my way. The spiritual path that I've chosen for myself is Tibetan Buddhism. . . . My hopes are that the surgery is successful from the perspective of my eyes on a physical level reflecting what I see from an internal perspective.

While the concept of harmony between inner self and outer is a staple in the contemporary aesthetic surgical imagination, the episode featuring Jodi Lang—a highly spiritualized and philosophical look at blepharoplasty—is noteworthy for its overt emphasis on what is implicit in all episodes of *A Personal Story*: this episode suggests that each patient's surgery can be tailored to her preexisting beliefs and preferences. Jodi speaks of her selected surgeon, Dr. Loren Eskenazi: "When I walked into her office and I saw that it had an Eastern decor to it, I was pleased, and that was my first sense of, wow, we might be at home here." Dr. Eskenazi tells us, "It's very important for me personally to get along with the patient in a way that I can understand them, where they've come from, how they're thinking, and I get an emotional rapport with them." While Dr. Eskenazi sees herself as the right surgeon for a range of different patients, she is also already largely in tune with Jodi's basic holistic lifestyle and belief system.

Dr. Eskenazi's basic position is that those who come in for surgery are going through some sort of transition, and that the surgery functions to "mark the transition." She asks Jodi whether, apart from the desire to have surgery, "there's anything else that's been going on." Jodi's "yes" prompts the doctor to elaborate, emphasizing a spiritual dimension that accords well with the aesthetic surgical industry's repeated stress on the ways in which surgery aligns inner and outer selves, being and becoming:

> My philosophy is basically that everybody who walks through the door to sit down and talk with me about doing something is going through some form of transition. You find out that a child's just left the nest, or they're having a relationship change. It's in my experience they're trying to mark the transition from the way they were to the way they're becoming.

Just before the day of surgery, Jodi offers a final affirmation that encapsulates the elements of optimism, social support, and rational choice that thread through all *Personal Stories:* "I really don't have any fears about this surgery. I feel very confident working with [Dr. Eskenazi]; I feel very relaxed with my friends supporting me. And again, I feel pretty balanced and mindful about this decision, and confident that all will go well."

On the day of surgery, Jodi and Dr. Eskenazi incorporate ritual into the process, setting up an altar containing icons meaningful to Jodi: both women light candles on Jodi's makeshift recovery room altar, which contains, in addition to candles, pictures of Buddhist figures and a tapestry. With these props, Jodi renders more explicit the quasi-religious appellation of the aesthetic surgical imaginary. Dr. Eskenazi speaks with Jodi about the significance of the various objects on her altar and acts with Jodi as a celebrant before surgery: "I dedicate this to your transition, seeing the world with clear eyes, through uncovered, clear vision." Following this segment, Dr. Eskenazi clarifies that while her medical practice is holistic, she herself is not locked into any specific path of spirituality, but allows patients to determine the shape of their experience for themselves: "It's not necessary that someone have, quote, a spiritual path in order to look at surgery this way. They could just become aware that they're involved with the healing process, so it doesn't have to be a fancy Tibetan ritual, or Native American ritual, or anything with any name or label on it. Jodi just happened to have one that she was already involved in."

Despite the carefully constructed appearance that all is harmonious in Jodi's life and cosmos as she looks toward her surgery, elements of abjection surface, and prompt us to notice their eruption throughout the episodes of *A Personal Story*. We learn that Jodi's concern about her eyes is not self-generated, but actually originated with her friend Ricki Polycove, who tells us that, "I'm the one who started her thinking about this." Ricki continues:

> I think Jodi is the kind of woman that you wouldn't expect to have plastic surgery, and I think I may be responsible for her having made the decision to have plastic surgery, because I commented on her eyes, and said, "You know, you don't have to live with that," and sort of got her thinking. . . . I think we're living in a wonderful time at very, very low risk, medically speaking, surgically speaking. We can have the appearance that in fact reflects how we feel about ourselves.

To some extent, then, Jodi's is a ventriloquized desire, informed by statements consistent with the advertisements by the aesthetic surgical industry that we have seen in earlier chapters, which assert that aligning inner and outer selves is a relatively unproblematic process. Ricki's role contradicts Jodi's assertion that she "went through many transitions, and this surgery marked the completion of these transitions," and that she is making her "own statement with [her] new eyes—being seen with new eyes, and seeing with new eyes." These statements serve as the incantations that organize and punctuate every segment of the episode, including the remarks of another friend, Horace Santry, whom Jodi talks into agreement:

> Jodi mentioned that she was having some medical work done. This surprised me because Jodi had never spoken about having any desires about changing her physical appearance. She'd always been relatively happy with how she looked. My first reaction was, well, Jodi doesn't need this, she's a beautiful woman. Everything's fine just the way it is. But as she spoke about this, and spoke specifically more about her eyes, I started to look at them, and about the third or fourth time I looked at them, I saw what she was talking about. And I started then to understand her rite of passage that she was talking about, having just finished her PhD program, and this program presenting, now that it's in completion and she is a doctor, a new identity, and the need for this new identity to also

have a face, to have a physical change. I think this change that she's going through is a way that will help Jodi to express deeply who she is.

The view that Jodi's eyes have not been able to "express deeply who she is," which began with the rather insistent remarks of a friend, becomes part of a reconstructed history of Jodi's own self-will. She tells us that "one of the most important roles that my friends play for me is that they *affirm* for me that what I'm doing is usually the right thing to be doing" (emphasis added). Unlike many other episodes of *A Personal Story*, this one reveals a sociocultural impetus for the decision, complicates the proposition that the patient is deciding for herself, and indicates that the decision may indeed entail the wish not to be abjected from social approval.

The second eruption of social bias occurs when Jodi is being prepared for surgery: Dr. Eskenazi measures Jodi's eyes, and marks the places where she will cut the eyelids. As the excisions are defined, Dr. Eskenazi's assistant says, in good humor, "There goes some more of Grandma." Earlier in the episode, we see a photograph of Jodi as a child, with her family, and Jodi speaks of her eyes having been inherited: "I'm aware that my eyes follow a lineage with my father and his mother, my grandmother." Dr. Eskenazi echoes her assistant, concurring, "There goes Grandma." Thus, at the same time that Jodi aims to attain a more harmonic relationship with the self she is becoming, she abjects the matriarchy that has defined her body.[10] The transition into "seeing with new eyes" and validating a better, truer, more authentic self is thus also a euphemism for the exiling of "Grandma," who of course represents the aged and the dead. In this case, Jodi has replaced the abject (Grandma) with a culturally constituted symbolic that merely pretends to a spirituality that can join the cosmological, historical, familial, communal, and psychological elements of the self.

The aesthetic surgical industry's ideology of patient self-determination downplays or disregards the abject body in culture even as it promises to intervene in a socioculturally determined condition. Dispensing with the possibility that it is inviting (more than simply receiving) persons into its care, the aesthetic surgical industry contributes to the real and perceived social decentralization that first drove the patient's desire to be surgically beautified. It brings patients into a new society, and distinguishes the reharmonized from those who have no "personal story" of aesthetic self-improvement to tell. But even within the well-scripted advertisements of the imaginary that make up the *Personal Story* series, abjection breaks out. The preference for being-in-oneself-as-oneself endorsed by the aesthetic surgical industry and serialized on *A Personal Story* is in tension with the proposition that one is responding to a world that informs our self-evaluations and decisions. To the extent that *A Personal Story* represents the prevailing epistemology and the hegemonic cultural imaginary, it allows patients to firmly adhere to a belief in the possibility of autonomy.

CHAPTER 5

Making Over Abjection

In 2000, the *Oprah Winfrey Show* had been the most popular program on daytime television for thirteen years (Twardowski 30, Squire 98), with its star an established cultural icon who, like Elvis and the Beatles, has become the subject of university courses studying her influence.[1] At the same time that Oprah Winfrey, as a black woman, belongs to the gender and race groupings of abject constituencies, she is also an emphatic representative of the aesthetic surgical imaginary in her dedication to the physical and psychological transformation of abjection into fulfilled selfhood. Within the Oprah philosophy, race and associated socioeconomic elements are curiously irrelevant to the pursuit of a makeover, which requires that one address the elements of powerlessness and despair by refusing all associations with victimage, and by extension, with abjection. Representing body-inner self integration as the continual theme of a tremendously popular television series, the 2000–2001 programs discussed in this chapter, along with the aphorisms and self-help exercises inculcated by *O, The Oprah Magazine*, feature the makeover as an explicit and preceptive goal, as the achievement of greater psychic health through body and attitude adjustments consistent with a total self-concept that emphasizes individual choice and responsibility. Thus, while Oprah Winfrey represents the continued popularity of the outside-in harmonic and the power of the autonomous individual, both valorized by the aesthetic surgical imaginary, she also skirts the desire for identification—the goal and result of objectification and abjection—as a culturally-sanctioned motive force in this process.

For Oprah, psychic health is associated with (1) maintaining a positive attitude, (2) living in the present, and (3) taking responsibility for one's choices. Each of these precepts is correlated with the care of the body and the development of a healthy body image, and supports the values and premises maintained by the aesthetic clinic.[2] By 2000, the *Oprah Winfrey Show* had come to sermonize, in the voice of a major pop culture icon, the features of the aesthetic surgical imaginary that we have surveyed to this point, idealizing the I-centered, positive-thinking, socially secure woman that the aesthetic surgical industry had been developing as its poster girl since the middle of the twentieth century in its efforts to bring the abject body into the marketplace.

Positive Thinking

Positive thinking grounds the ongoing makeover project, to the extent that makeovers are necessarily motivated by trust in the possibility of improvement. *O, The Oprah Magazine*, which debuted in spring 2000, becomes aggressively aphoristic on this score, with large, multiarticle sections titled "Dream It, Do It" and "Enjoy Yourself" (September 2000), "Trust Yourself" (October 2000), and "Live Your Best Life" (November 2000), each issue including an "Oprah to Go" section that features brief sayings printed on illustrated cards that are perforated to allow for readers to tear them out and carry them around. As the "Oprah to Go" title suggests, the sayings are associated with the consumption of Oprah's own spirit by her readers, and become species of the host (in both the religious and media-oriented uses of that term). The "Oprah To Go" menu includes Shirley MacLaine; "I could be whatever I wanted to be if I trusted that music, that song, that vibration of God that was inside of me" ("Words You Can Trust," October 2000, 141); Marcel Proust: "Let us be grateful to people who make us happy: They are the charming gardeners who make our souls blossom" ("A Place for Thanks Giving," November 2000, 122); and one of Oprah's personal discoveries, Ron Rathburn, who writes, "What you find in your mind is what you put there. Put good things in there" ("Words To Grow On," September 2000, 141).

These aphorisms coincide with injunctions to synchronize inner self and outer and the idea that body image is self-constructed. The October 2000 feature in *O* called "Mirror Image" (Breathnach) typifies Oprah's belief in the reciprocity of inner and outer self. Proposing, "If you say nice things to your mirror, your mirror will say nice things to you," this article describes the daily ritual of standing before a full-length mirror and giving oneself compliments ("I love the color of my eyes. I love how my hair curls behind my ear. I love my long neck. I love my toes.") in order to develop an acceptance and appreciation of ones body: "I am what I am, and what I am is wonderful" (202). This sort of exercise is not inconsistent with scholarly reconsiderations of body image that recognize it as a multivariant phenomenon significantly affected by "internal, subjective representations" (Cash and Pruzinsky xi), and recognizes implicitly what is stated more explicitly elsewhere in the Oprah canon: that individual will can be an effective counter to oppressive body ideals. However, the Mirror Image exercise also functions to ritualize the repression of abjection. Notably, this exercise is illustrated with the photograph of an attractive young blonde woman standing in her underwear before a full-length mirror, thus confusing the acceptance and admiration of one's body with the desire for conventional beauty that is, for most women, unfulfilled. Abjection is displaced by the picture of youth in a body that has no frailties: "When you look in the mirror, reframe how you describe yourself: My legs are powerful. My arms are strong. My stomach is soft and cuddly. My hips are womanly."

Gail Weiss's work on the need for new models of normal and abnormal bodies concludes, with reference to Kristevan abjection, that "that which is 'lost' or which resists incorporation into the body image is also precisely what makes the coherent body image possible because it marks the boundary between the body image and what is not" (89). In the context of the makeover culture that Oprah enfranchises, the features that disrupt a mature conception of body image are those that reference clinical realities and resist or make impossible a makeover: weakness, asymmetry, infertility, disproportion, age, sagging, disease, anger, fear, sadness. Thus, Oprah finds her success models in those who have left the incoherent, abject body behind: Elie Wiesel is featured in *O* as someone who "survived the Holocaust with his sanity—and his heart—intact" ("Oprah Talks with Elie Wiesel," November 2000, cover), whose year 2000 portrait as an elegant man in a pinstripe suit is printed adjacent to and four times larger than a 1945 picture of him lying among emaciated comrades in Buchenwald, the current portrait representing the possibility—within the context of this magazine—of moving from the horrors of nazi fascism to normalcy, going on, as Wiesel puts it, "to love beautiful girls, to talk, to write, to have toast and tea and live my life" (234). Serious traumas, or in this case, unspeakable terrors, come to represent a transitional stage to a mature view of the body that is peaceful, purposeful, accomplished.

Indeed, one of the signal marks of the transition away from what is not part of a coherent self-image is the refusal of victimage. One repeated guest on the *Oprah Winfrey Show* has been Gary Zukav, a popular contemporary proponent of the power of attitude management, who declares what has become central to the popular philosophy that Oprah represents: "There are no such things as victims" (February 10, 2000). There are, instead, hurtful experiences that (1) may not always be comprehensible in a meaningful way, because they are part of a large and mysterious extrasensory realm; and (2) may actually provide the opportunity for drawing a constructive lesson or a new appreciation of one's life. The rejection of victimage coincides with the rejection of an externalized self that identifies with the expectations of others, a self that may, through affliction by what Zukav calls the "disease to please," suffer a sense of fragmentation and incoherence. "Tracey" on the "Lifestyle Makeovers" show expresses this view:

> My life is very chaotic. It's chaotic because everything kind of blends and blurs together. I work at home and I also watch my daughter. I do my chores in the middle of the day. Well, I may be doing laundry talking on the phone to some editor, making grilled cheese. I feel like I do everything halfway. I'm half of a good wife, I'm half of a good mother. I'm half of a good worker, and I feel like I'm nothing to myself. I'm empty on that side. (May 29, 2000)

The advice for Tracey is to quit the victimage and prioritize her individual needs, putting her "emotional, physical, and spiritual well-being" first. Psychological normalcy and fulfillment require the unitary coherence of the individual, through the exclusion of the "not me," in a transition from inarticulate pain to a forcibly aphoristic makeover of a happy ego in a beautiful body.

UPDATING AND UPGRADING

People's resistance to being made over is associated with living in the past, a state often described in infantilizing terms, as in this daughter's description of her father as a child of the 1960s who refuses to grow up:

> I was born in the '70s, and I know that he wears suits from way before I was born. My dad has this purple suit. He wears these awful purple shoes, purple socks. He has a matching hat to go with every one of his suits. He thinks he's hip, but he's not. So, Oprah, can you please help my dad? (January 3, 2000).

While one kind of Oprah-approved mindset advises growing past fragmentation and pain by excluding external valuative forces, another advises that we modify our looks to suit current fashion trends, and suggests that not doing so is regressive, and that it contributes to unhappiness. The purple-suited dad is "stuck in the '70s," one of a number of people Oprah has located who are living "in a time warp."[3]

The aesthetic surgical industry advances the same paradox and contradictions that are maintained in the articulation of the spiritual and fashion makeovers, promoting both the externalization of a genuine, hidden, and repressed self that is uncompromised by cultural pressures and ideals and conformity to current beauty ideals. Just so, the potential candidate for dermabrasion or a breast lift is enjoined to bridge the gap between an aging body and a youthful state of mind, thus matching her appearance more closely to her authentic interior self, while she is also told that better relationships and higher incomes come to those with youthful good looks. Not surprisingly, one element of Oprah's "Millennium Makeovers" is aesthetic surgery: "Edna's backstage right now getting her makeover. . . . We even arranged to have the mole removed from her lip. . . . [I]t is something that Edna was born with and it's bothered her her whole life." The emphasis on both prioritizing individual needs and redressing oneself to please the eyes of one's beholders would seem to recommend two contradictory kinds of happiness. But the operative vision that mitigates contradiction is holistic: appearance makeovers should be pursued in conformity with one's general self-improvement, so that one's present body reflects one's best self, a self that may have been obscured even from one's own consciousness. After one woman changes the hairstyle and color she's had for thirty years, Oprah says, "And look at your hair bouncing around now. Don't you just feel bouncier?"—to which the guest responds, "Oh, yeah, I've never had bounce before." Body makeovers evoke moods, attitudes, and energies that might otherwise have lain dormant. Appearance is an expression of soul, and bringing them together under the sign of beauty is a high achievement, as Oprah notes when she characterizes Annie Leibovitz (guesting in a segment on the "Millennium Makeovers" show) as a photographer who makes people "look extraordinary and also feel like themselves."

FREEDOM OF CHOICE

Making choices is the most important thing that you do in your life. It doesn't matter what your circumstances in life are. If you have three children and a husband who's left, if you've just lost your job, it doesn't matter if you're educated or you're not educated. One thing that you have in your life and will always have is choice. . . . You are not a prisoner of your circumstances. You are a creator of your circumstances.

—Gary Zukav, *The Oprah Winfrey Show,* "Choose Your Life," June 21, 2000

This address by Zukav, at the conclusion of a show featuring those who have abandoned certain careers or lifestyles for others that represent, in the guests' words, the fulfillment of dreams, is reinforced by Oprah's full approval: "I think what Gary said could not be more of the truth for everybody, no matter where you are in your life, in your space, right now." We tend to regard freedom of choice as an essential liberty, and the ability to make good choices as an element of a prosperous selfhood. For Oprah, personal choices determine the quality of one's life, and recognizing this can be part of one's emergence from crisis into instrumental consciousness: choice responsibility is thus a crucial component of the "made-over" person. This choice responsibility extends not only to matters such as lifestyle, career, and body image, but also to controlling what might otherwise be regarded as traumatic and severely tragic events. One guest, Jody, describes the death of her newborn child Ryan to Oprah and Zukav, and asks, "How do I not let this loss and tragedy in my life take it over?":

> Zukav: This is a matter of perspective. . . . Every soul comes into
> the Earth school when it *chooses*. And every personality or
> soul leaves the Earth school when it *chooses*. . . . You will
> reach a place in your life where you are grateful that this
> soul *chose* to be with you for however short a time. . . .
> [emphasis added]
> Winfrey: That's pretty powerful. That is pretty powerful. That is
> pretty powerful. . . . (January 4, 2001)

The power and comfort associated with Ryan's death are founded in the belief that souls, and by extension the individuals that house them, can and do choose the nature and quality of their existence, and that realizing this takes a transformative shift in perspective, away from identification with victimage, tragedy, and fear.

The occasional examples of dealing with death, loss, and rape are addressed within the same philosophical celebration of choice that applies to much less drastic events, so that it becomes a universal prescription for a wide spectrum of psychoemotional suffering, a central ingredient of any makeover, from the refashioning of one's wardrobe to the exertion of power over mortality. Integral to the makeover concept is the belief that everyone is able to choose a better life, and that the lifestyle makeover is an equal opportunity phenomenon:

> Winfrey: OK. So you all know I want to use television to do
> whatever I can to improve other people's lives. . . . You can

> begin to find out for yourself, not just as a voyeuristic—you know, looking at somebody else's life—how to begin to reorder your own, so that it begins to work for you and allows you to experience what I say . . . in my new magazine the—the possibility of living your best life. I believe everybody has the ability to do that. . . . That's how we're created equal. (May 29, 2000)

With her implicit reference here to the Constitutional right to the pursuit of happiness, Oprah translates that right into an ability to improve one's life that corresponds with the ability to make choices. The original declaration of a right to the pursuit of happiness was, of course, a response to oppressive governmental circumstances, written as a call for political revolution. Making it a right that is also a responsibility removes the element of unfair treatment, and also suggests that those who do not choose to live their "best life" are living in a deliberate state of abjection, and so become lifestyle makeover outlaws.[4]

Those who wish to reform their outlaw status are often cast in the role of the penitent on shows that follow a confessional format in which guests admit to culpability in their own unhappiness:

> Winfrey: So you make choices in life. That's what we're talking about. Well, when Marcy Anderson's weight reached an all-time high of 405 pounds, she also made a choice, a decision.
> Ms. Anderson: I was a fat girl all my life. I made a choice to eat my way to 400 pounds. . . . Then I made a choice to change my life once and for all. . . . Fourteen months later, I had lost 270 pounds. . . .
> Winfrey: And it was a choice?
> Ms. Anderson: It was definitely a choice. It was a choice to stay alive. (June 21, 2000)

At the same time that the suffering individual should develop an independent, self-specific will to improve, without assessing her plight in terms of victimage or continuing to externalize her self-worth, she is also encouraged to regard the celebrity and beauty industries as allies in her self-improvement, benevolent and devoted forces that seem to both set mass criteria for beauty and accomplishment and assist individuals in heeding their inner voices:

> Winfrey: And a special thank-you to Kieva Spa for making our guests look so great. (February 2, 2000)

> We even arranged to have the mole removed from her upper lip by Dr. Randall McNally . . . who does plastic and reconstructive surgery at Rush-Presbyterian-St. Luke's Medical Center here in Chicago. . . . Andre and Reggie did your makeup. That's great. I want to thank the whole team from Frederic Fekkai, too. (January 3, 2000)
>
> And Jesse Garza from Visual Therapy—visualtherapy.com. . . . He takes a look at the women, and then he goes out and he finds the perfect outfit for them. (November 11, 2000)
>
> Thank-you, Ivan Noel Salon in Chicago and Marshall Field's for helping us transform Lia, Emily, and Judy into age-defying women. (May 5, 2000)

Good mental health, then, entails a certain trust in corporate benevolence that coincides with the prioritizing of individual needs, and the belief that success or failure is a consequence of one's own choices, rather than cooperation with other forces. It follows, then, that those who suffer from low self-esteem or exhibit indications that they are not leading their "best lives," have chosen not to grow up into the opportunity that could be theirs. Within a cultural atmosphere that increasingly sees aesthetic surgery as affordable, available, and effective, the choice not to have a surgical makeover will be more and more striking and odd.

At the same time that the availability and perceived accessibility and normalcy of aesthetic body modification increasingly makes denying its benefits the wrong choice, aesthetic surgery is alone among medical interventions in which the patient gets to choose both her condition and her treatment. Sander Gilman has recognized that "aesthetic surgery demands the putative autonomy of the individual . . . as the grounding for any choice as to how his or her body is to be altered" (*Creating Beauty* 21–22). However, choice turns out to be something of an illusion, since outcomes do not promote diversity but uniformity and resemblance. In this connection, Gilman makes a distinction between aesthetic surgery and psychoanalysis:

Aesthetic surgery is composed of those surgical interventions that claim that the acquisition of an idealized or imagined body type or physiognomy is a "cure" for "unhappiness." This is very different from Sigmund Freud's claims for psychoanalysis, which hopes, at best, to transform "your hysterical misery into common unhappiness" (*Creating Beauty* 24).

Thus, aesthetic surgery promises more than psychotherapy, and while psychotherapy seeks initiation of the patient into a greater psychic health defined as the acceptance of the imperfect self through regression, aesthetic surgery encourages regression as both a means and an end, and associates mental health with the resistance to imperfection and the assertion of a uniqueness that defies one's personal history of ordinary physical and psychological vulnerability.

It is disturbingly ironic that the utility of abjection to allow recognition of a multiplicity of possible and existent bodies is repressed in both popular philosophy and the aesthetic clinic as a substitute plurality, of choices, within a concept of choice in the service of management, removal of excess, uniformity, regression, and the incorporation of preceptive and instrumental rationality. The second annual edition of "Plastic Surgery Today," an eight-page advertising supplement to *USA Today* published by the American Society of Plastic Surgeons, features the availability and importance of choice at three stages of the aesthetic surgical process: defining what needs to be fixed, deciding how to fix it, and selecting the right surgeon to do the job. It is significant, for instance, that breast reconstruction is featured repeatedly as "a woman's choice," dramatically linking aesthetic surgery to procedures performed as a result not of choice, but of the vulnerability of the body to disease. Consequential to a body out of control there is the promise of restoration, of regression to precancerous life, with a breast that "looks, feels, and moves like a natural breast" (1). Though most people do not think that reconstructive breast surgery is unwarranted, it is nonetheless significant that this surgical choice is featured with emphasis on the volitional management of body and mind that are also central to more fully elective procedures:

> Plastic surgery is the art and science of reshaping the body—whether it's for cosmetic improvement like a facelift or to correct congenital body deformities like cleft lip and palate, or to reconstruct the body after trauma or other surgery, like breast reconstruction for women after mastectomy. The same physician who can put a child's face back together after a brutal dog attack may also be the one to perform liposuction on you or your spouse. (1)

It is difficult to miss the implication that one's facelift is a contribution to a less monstrous world, so that the luxury of means and choice is implicitly associated with an ethical imperative.

The victim of breast cancer has limited choice over what needs fixing, but for others, the scope of the menu indicates both the exercise of personal liberty and the susceptibility of the body to hyperrational modification. The center page of "Plastic Surgery Today" features side-by-side drawings of a sans-genital nude man and a nude woman without nipples or pubic hair as maps of the possible sites for aesthetic surgery; taken together they represent the range of the most popular correctives, and considered separately they represent, incidentally, the maintenance of traditional gendered formations of desire. The woman has arrows drawn to her breasts and her thighs as potential problem areas; the man has arrows drawn only to his face to target the possibility of eyelid surgery, facelift, and rhinoplasty. The general effect is emphasis on the brain-proximate areas of the male, and for the female, the sexualized parts. Thus the availability of surgical choices, while not exclusively limited to one sex or the other, is featured so as to maintain both heterosexuality and the hegemony of the masculinized intellect.

The explicit purpose of the "Plastic Surgery Today" insert is, however, to advertise the option of choosing what to fix and to present those choices as relatively simple schematics:

Facelift (Rhytidectomy)

Purpose: To rejuvenate the appearance of the face by tightening the skin (and sometimes the muscles) of the face, chin, and neck.

How it's done: Working through incisions hidden behind the hair-line, excess facial fat is removed and muscles are tightened.

Recovery: Patients typically return to work within two weeks. Most of the bruising and swelling subsides after 2–3 weeks.

Staying power: Facelifts may last up to 10 years.

Liposuction (Suction-Assisted Lipectomy)

Purpose: To improve the contour of the body, face, neck, arms and/or legs.

How it's done: Exercise-resistant pockets of fat are suctioned from the body with a tube and vacuum device.

Recovery: Most people are back to work within two weeks, but need to avoid strenuous activity for about a month. The final result may not be visible until several months have passed and the swelling subsides.

Staying power: Permanent, with sensible diet and exercise. (3)

The simplification of choice through the "at a glance" description obviously contributes to the commodification of surgical choice as a relatively straightforward process, complementary to the choice of a surgeon, which is described as a three-step process: (1) gathering names, (2) Checking credentials, and (3) the consultation. The basic process is no different from what one might employ in the selection of a babysitter, and in that sense, features the mechanics of choice as common coin and a resistance to choosing as the inability to carry out even the simplest of deliberative exercises.

Altogether, the three behaviors that for Oprah constitute successful living—positive attitude, living in the present, and taking responsibility for one's choices—comprise a celebration of agency and volition, stressing the ways in which an operationalized will can alter material circumstances. Abjection, then, becomes a kind of lapse in determination, or the consequence of sloppy self-management. Blaming those who do not shape up is nothing new; as a staple of conservative social and political philosophy, it has allowed for a rights-based valorization of the individual. But now, such a philosophy is reinforced by advances in medical technology that encourage more optimistic views of health and longevity, advances in information processing and formatting that support tendencies toward the schematic and simplified presentation of complex material, and the growing perception through the 1990s and into the early twenty-first century of a rising middle class of baby boomers that is accumulating greater wealth and buying power.

PASSING

"Passing" is most familiar in connection with light-skinned blacks like Peola in Fannie Hurst's *Imitation of Life*, whose difference is invisible to the white race. It takes on broader significance at this cultural moment, when the popular emphasis on freedom of choice is bolstered by the widespread advertisement of technologies for amending the body, so that aging persons can pass for persons much younger, and those with conspicuously ethnic physical features can have them moderated. As Sander Gilman notes, "We "pass" in order to regain control of ourselves and to efface that which is seen as different, which marks us as visible in the world. Relieving the anxiety of being placed into a visible, negative category, aesthetic surgery provides relief from imagining oneself as a stereotype" (*Making the Body Beautiful* 331). Though the emphasis may be on creating a distinctive, individualized identity, preset standards of beauty and the standardized procedures used to achieve them mean a greater uniformity of physical appearances. The best result one can hope for is not recognition as an individual, but rather, the invisibility that comes with group identification, with blending into a mass popular aesthetic that rejects features like purple clothes and big hair, physical feebleness and deterioration, non-Caucasian traits—what Toni Morrison calls "funkiness" in *The Bluest Eye*—fat, and wrinkles. Absent these qualities, one passes.

In an *Oprah Winfrey Show* based on Leah Feldon's makeover guide, *Does This Make Me Look Fat?* (February 23, 2001), a series of women describe various kinds of disproportionate body mass distribution (a "life preserver" stomach, "saddleback" thighs, thick calves, "sausage" arms). Pam Calloway, thirty-four-year-old black nurse, complains about her "ethnic butt," confessing that she's a size 6 on the top and a 12 on the bottom, and displaying herself in a video in which she appears in overtight denim jeans that emphasize her wide hips. Leah Feldon notes that Pam, like many women, is "unbalanced," and rebalances her with a new outfit that adds mass to her upper half with a padded bra and shoulder pads, and hides her "ethnic butt" with a long black cardigan sweater over a long black skirt. The repeated message is that women can choose to efface distinctive body traits by dressing strategically and thus passing as "balanced." The use of "unbalanced" as a repeated problem designation maintains the connection between physical features and mental health, insofar as a primary denotation of unbalanced is "mentally disordered" or "deranged," and also designates a body out of control, ranging outside the boundaries of the acceptable dimensions established within a classical Eurocentric aesthetic.

Pam's particular predicament recalls the well-known nineteenth-century celebrity of the "Hottentot Venus." Sartje Baartman was a native African exhibited as a freak in London and Paris from 1810 to 1815 because of her supposed disproportionately large buttocks. The buttocks were considered indicators of hidden and equally excessive genitalia: "Baartman's notorious buttocks and genitalia became an icon for dangerously excessive and grotesque female sexuality, simultaneously embodying the opposite of supposedly domesticated, European female sexuality and warning of what that sexuality might become if not rigorously managed" (Thomson 72). The incorrect but prevailing association of Baartman with the Hottentot tribe reinforced her identification as a deviant alien, and rumors about her overdeveloped clitoris "reflects the general nineteenth-century understanding of female sexuality as pathological" and contributes to a persistent stereotyping of large-hipped black women (*Disease and Representation* 88).[5] When Pam Calloway describes the ridicule she has suffered because of her "ethnic butt," she places herself within the tradition of enfreakment that we see in the treatment of Baartman. When Oprah stages Pam's makeover, she implicitly, albeit unwittingly, participates in this tradition, joining the derogation of racial difference with the insistence that black women can and should choose to pass as other than the Hottentot.[6]

The abjection hidden and, to all eyes, "healed" by redressing the Hottentot in a long black sweater and skirt is a condition that Oprah will occasionally recall as a personal experience: in a program devoted to Toni Morrison's *The Bluest Eye* (May 26, 2000), Oprah recounts a childhood reminiscent of Morrison's Pecola, in which Oprah's grandmother chastised Oprah daily while she talked of the white family she worked for "with pleasure." Echoing Morrison's themes, Oprah concurs that she saw her body as less lovable than a white one: "You can be loved more if you're white. If I were only white, she would love me more." Morrison is interested not only in the racism, or "colorism," that originates in white culture, but also in how that bias or favoritism becomes internalized within the black community. The sort of learned delight in whiteness and disgust for blackness that *Bluest Eye*'s Claudia tells us she has partly internalized manifests itself in the preference within the black community itself for light skin color. Maureen Peal, a schoolmate of Claudia and her sister Frieda, is a light-skinned black: "A high-yellow dream child . . . as rich as the richest of white girls . . . [with] sloe green eyes . . . [and a taste for] white milk," who, unlike the other girls, does not get tripped by black boys in the halls (62–63). Maureen admires the movie character Peola, played by Rochelle Hudson in the 1934 *Imitation of Life,* a light-skinned black who passes for white, thinking her "so pretty," unlike Peola's mother (played by Louise Beavers) who is "black and ugly" (67). It is clear that Maureen sees her own situation in the film (she tells us that her mother "has seen [the film] four times" 68) and that the favoritism she enjoys from others is a form of "passing." Morrison's Pecola differs dramatically from the film's Peola: she does not have the luxury to pass as white, but is destined for destruction within a cultural system of values that denies her dignity.

The novel's lesson for Oprah, of the error of women defining themselves "by what other people think of them," leads by a certain logic to her repeated insistence upon the cultivation of individual power rather than the resignation to categorical victimage; however, that lesson also becomes transformed, distorted, into the concept of the makeover,[7] which strategically links individual desire with the accession to aesthetic conformity.[8] The transmutation of abjection into the lifestyle makeover is, ironically, a reinscription of Pecola's insane delusion that she had been given blue eyes, a reinscription into squeals of delight by women coming on camera in their new outfits, who behave as if the momentary concealment of the racial body is both permanent and wonderful.

Morrison's focus on American commodity culture through Pecola's and Frieda's enamorment of Shirley Temple and Claudia's rejection of white baby dolls given as Christmas presents to little black girls puts us in mind of the celebration of choice, individuality, power, control, and normalcy that has found its contemporary image in Mattel's Barbie doll.[9] Barbie has been internationalized into a figure that can pass through a transnational, transracial, transprofessional array of identities with the same basic set of features, enclosing and foreclosing all difference. The impossibility of her body (with tiny feet and a massive chest that would cause any real woman to topple over like an inverted pear), and the distortion of diversity she promotes have not compromised her iconic status. Certainly she has been parodied as an extreme and unrealistic example of the perfected aesthetic body in Carl Hiaasen's novel *Sick Puppy*, which follows a ruthless Florida land developer's obsession with turning a pair of Scandinavian models into twin Barbies through a series of aesthetic surgeries, and in a 1999 episode of the medical drama *Chicago Hope* ("Oh What a Piece of Work Is Man"), featuring a character who desperately desires just one more surgical procedure to perfect her Barbie features: double-D breast implants.[10] At the same time, she remains the toy product that most widely represents to generations of women and girls the worldwide status of women, through an array of dolls that includes Doctor Barbie and Astronaut Barbie among the "professional" collection, and Nigerian Barbie and Arctic Barbie in the large "international" collection.

Reverence for Barbie's cultural ambassadorship became institutionalized in South Florida with the 1999 opening of "Forty Years of the Barbie Doll"[11] at the Cornell Museum in Delray Beach. The exhibit not only presents eighty international Barbie dolls donated from private collections, but also offers credit in "multicultural training" toward the certification of present or prospective Florida schoolteachers. For credit, teachers visit the exhibit, observe Nigerian Barbie in her arm bracelets and Arctic Barbie in her parka, and tell in writing how the dolls will affect their teaching. The Barbies display a range of skin tones, but each has the same button nose, slim waist, and Caucasian hair, and the doll boxes on display typically limit cultural education to assuring children that this apparent foreigner who might usually be regarded as strange and threatening is really friendly, and a source of interesting expressions and customs: "We live in the beautiful cold lands of the Arctic," and "'Chimo' in Eskimo means 'Hello, I'm friendly, are you friendly?'" The curator stresses the pedagogical value of what she understands as Barbie's authenticity: "If I want to teach someone about Brazil, what's more interesting—having them read an article in the encyclopedia or using an animated figure like a Barbie doll to teach the true facts?" (Pickel 1D). To those who object that the international Barbies do not have ethnic features, she says that

Barbie cannot be changed too dramatically, or "it wouldn't be Barbie" (1D). A Black woman visiting the museum notes that "Barbie has been able to transcend all time and cultures. That's what we look at—inclusiveness. Barbie kind of captured the market on that" (5D).[12] The museum also features televisions running video tapes of the 1970s sitcom "Julia," which featured Diahann Carroll in the first starring television role for a black woman; the implication is that Carroll, whose features correspond with Caucasian beauty, counts as one of the multicultural Barbies, another beautiful professional woman of color without prominent racial markers.

To the extent that a successful life of self-care is dependent on the cultivation and concerted obedience to "good thoughts," Barbie gives us someone to think about as we make ourselves over and as we develop an ethics that acknowledges the importance of diversity while it centralizes the desire to become, as Sander Gilman suggests, so normalized that one is invisible. Ann duCille has noted that the Barbie image reinforces an "easy pluralism":

> Made from essentially the same mould as what Mattel considers its signature doll—the traditional, blonde, blue-eyed Barbie—tawny-tinted ethnic reproductions are both signs and symptoms of an easy pluralism that simply melts down and adds on a reconstituted other without transforming the established social order, without changing the mould. (112)[13]

Finally, the goal of body image modification is a psychosurgically achieved invisibility that aligns passing with the adaptation to an industry mold. We see this at the level of spectacle in the Miss Universe pageant, where an array of native costumes is hung on what amounts to the same, Barbie-esque body, so that Miss Botswana, Miss South Africa, Miss India, and Miss Venezuela all say, "Hello, I'm friendly" through their homogeneity. The pageant has astutely internationalized the anglocentric beauty of the Caucasian West, where the international body becomes not only a determined and uniform version of beauty, but also an image that excludes, or more to the point, graphically excises from public approbation, all the other female bodies in Botswana, South Africa, and India. All of those others, while they are not yet psychosurgically adapted to the invisibility that gains one entry to the larger cultural pageant of acceptable bodies, remain what Arthur Kroker and Michael Weinstein call "surplus flesh" (84).

HAPPY AGING

To the extent that aging and death are not choices, a limit that often also applies to poverty and disability, they are not amenable to the calculus of consumerist rationality, yet this reality is suppressed in the aesthetic surgical imaginary through a lexicon of empowerment stressing that choosing against abjection is good for every body. This lexicon is a staple of trade books on aesthetic surgery and issues from a larger atmosphere, emblematized in popular forums like the Learning Channel's *A Personal Story*, the *Oprah* phenomenon, and, as I will indicate below, from the official voice of aging Americans, the American Association of Retired Persons. Through all of these venues, we learn repeatedly that (1) the mind is free to make choices that improve the body; (2) the ills of the body are largely constructed by the mind (so that even pain in death is to some considerable degree psychosomatic); and (3) those who are not preparing to make and making choices that defy aging, death, poverty, and disability (you mean you haven't had a face lift yet? Don't you think you should learn some pain management/money management/career management/age management techniques?) are sadly, but not sympathetically, unfortunate.

In 2000, *Modern Maturity* was the most widely circulated magazine in America, having long held that distinction. Published by the American Association of Retired Persons, *Modern Maturity* is sent to over twenty million AARP members (with a qualifying age for membership of fifty), maintaining wide regard as a definitive representation of both the audience it serves and the concept it names. Its determined association of post-fifty life with control over the fortunes of the body constitutes a refutation of abjection that foregrounds rejuvenation, self-management strategies, and financial security, themes at the forefront of aesthetic surgical consciousness. In 1999–2000, *Modern Maturity* underwent a makeover with a series of ten bimonthly issues that established an ideology that would lead, in spring 2001, to a further rejuvenation of the magazine and its target audience. The nine new-millennial issues are my focus here, beginning with a July/August 1999 issue whose cover features supermodel Cheryl Tiegs, a markedly vibrant-looking fifty-year-old, as the first of a series of *Modern Maturity* poster children for a first-rate sunset half of life: Susan Sarandon, Sophia Loren, Sean Connery, Paul McCartney, Judith Sheindlin (television's "Judge Judy"), and television journalist Cokie Roberts.

Each issue in this millennial period treats a central theme in a series of related feature articles:

July/August 1999: Fitness

September/October 1999: Great Sex

November/December 1999: Longevity

January/Feb 2000: Rejuvenation
March/April 2000: Creativity
May/June 2000: Vietnam/the Military
July/August 2000: Money
September/October 2000: Death
November/December 2000: The Presidential Election

These themes maintain a predominant emphasis on what makes for happy aging. Even the issues on the subject of the military (subdued by an upbeat article on "The 50 Most Alive Places to Live") and on the election (bypassing any hard-edged discussion of issues that affect seniors—social security, prescription drug benefits—for relatively light treatments such as the views of celebrity pundits and wish-list letters to the new president by well-known columnists) focus largely on entertainment.

The fall 2000 issue on death seems a significant departure, given that death is the very negation of fitness, great sex, longevity, rejuvenation, and the pleasures that money can buy (even the strong defense of life, liberty, and so on that is the job of the military). However, the issue on death puts forth a curious and significant resistance to dying, so that this process, improperly experienced, is the definitive capitulation to abjection. In the pages of *Modern Maturity*, dying becomes, alternatively, the last opportunity to customize one's life, by creating conditions for "The Good Death." Here is part of the introduction to the "special pull-out section" on preparing for death:

> The new movement to improve the end of life is pioneering ways to make available to each of us a good death—as we each define it. One goal of the movement is to bring death through the cultural process that childbirth has achieved; from an unconscious, solitary act in a cold hospital room to a situation in which one is buffered by pillows, pictures, music, loved ones, and the solaces of home. But as in the childbirth movement, the real goal is choice—here, to have the death you want. *Much of death's sting can be averted by planning in advance, knowing the facts, and knowing what options we all have.* In this handbook, we have gathered new and relevant information to help us all make a difference for the people we are taking care of, and ultimately, for ourselves. (Matousek 52, emphasis added)

As Sherwin Nuland establishes at length in *How We Die*, and as Robert Frost reminds us in "Provide, Provide" when he writes that nothing "keeps the end from being hard," death's "sting" is likely, and very painful.[14] It is striking, in view of the reality of death as the ultimate loss of all control, that *Modern Maturity* takes a managerial position, essentially saying that mental preparedness is the key to controlling the riot of the body, advocating the same virtues that apply, for instance, to buying mutual funds—factual knowledge and planning—and maintaining the mythology of the preeminence of the disembodied self over physical breakdown. Against the likelihood of great pain, and setting aside the fact that no one of us knows with any fullness or certainty what a dying person feels, *Modern Maturity* propagates the *ars moriendi* in the categorical language of hyperrationality:

> Fear of pain . . . is one of the most common problems, and can be dealt with rationally. Many people do not know, for example, that pain in dying is not inevitable. Other typical fears are of being separated from loved ones, from home, from work; fear of being a burden, losing control, being dependent, and leaving things undone. Voicing fear helps lessen it, and pinpointing fear helps a caregiver know how to respond. (54)

Sections titled "Take Control Now," "Designing the Care You Want," and "Filing, Storing, Safekeeping" continue to proffer the model of a failing body whose abjection is subjugated by reason, determination, and orderliness. Those who do not die well in this era of custom deaths, then, have only themselves to blame.

It is no surprise that managerial behaviors are prompted by the experience of abjection; technologies for taking categorical approaches to chaotic processes constitute, in themselves, an aesthetics that defines popular Western culture. The urgency to manage aging, disease, and disability is now especially rife among baby boomers, so that those who were drawn to aerobic conditioning and fitness-center culture as thirty-somethings in the 1980s become beneficiaries of widely available anti-aging regimens and procedures in the new millenium. Today's drugstores stock Melatonin and DHEA (whose depletion is associated with aging and deterioration), Rogaine for male pattern baldness; alpha hydroxy for wrinkles, and phytochemicals to ward off cancer, grow new hair, and increase energy. Mainstream vitamin companies such as Centium and One-A-Day feature a line of herbal supplements previously available only in health food stores: gingko biloba for improved memory, ginseng for energy, saw palmetto for prostate health, garlic for cholesterol reduction, echinacea for immune system strength, St. John's wort for stress relief. Soft drink manufacturers that include PepsiCo and Coca-Cola have brought out "nutraceutical" beverages that feature anti-aging, fat-burning, and immunity-enhancing supplements in fruit-flavored drinks such as Elations with glucosamine, believed to slow cartilage erosion, and SoBe Lean, advertised as "liquid liposuction" because it contains a fruit (garcinia cambogia) that may inhibit fat synthesis. Coca-Cola's CEO has called Elations "youth in a bottle," and in concert with so many advertisements that proclaim that "aging is optional" and "aging is a treatable disease" ("Clinical studies") states flatly that he is responding to a clear and widespread desire: "Baby boomers don't want to grow old" (Barnes and Winter 14).[15]

Gary Null, producer of a Public Broadcasting program titled *How To Live Forever* and numerous compendious books on better health and appearance, declares in the *Ultimate Anti-Aging Program* that the advances in understanding and treating aging construct a new vision of normalcy:

> Hypertension, congestive heart disease, arterial sclerosis, stroke, dementia, arthritis, diabetes, Parkinson's, Alzheimer's, cancer, osteoporosis; menopause; graying and hair loss; wrinkled skin, fatigue; weakness; loss of muscle mass and tone; diminishing vision, smell, and hearing; a tendency to overweight; digestive problems, and loss of appetite—I refuse to accept these conditions as normal. (4)

Null typifies a popular conviction that the body is becoming ever more resilient, more powerful, and more adaptable to an active life in a posthuman world in which biophysical upgrades lie within reach of the realistic imagination. Contemporary technological solutions to the troubles of the flesh, while contributing to a genuine decrease in people's suffering, also promote the view that the aged body is an unnecessary deviation from the good body.

At the same time that it urges managerial control, *Modern Maturity* repeatedly acknowledges physical matters over which we have no choice, primarily degenerative disease. Significantly, such acknowledgments are almost always restricted to paid advertisements, with banners such as "Is it just forgetfulness . . . or Alzheimer's disease?" Such conditions are inimical to a makeover, but well within the sphere of therapeutic or corrective technologies ("Aricept" for Alzheimer's, or the "Video Eye Magnification System" for macular degeneration). Such advertisements stand apart from the celebrity vitality featured on *Modern Maturity* covers and the feature articles devoted to the productive management of longevity. Further, while the feature articles are largely aimed at a readership in its fifties populated by individuals who can identify more readily with recommendations for a vigorous and optimistic lifestyle, older and weaker people, past the conventional retirement age of sixty-five, are the targets of product sales rather than advice. Appeals to this audience set aside the *Oprah Winfrey Show* emphasis on positive thinking as a way to improve physical conditions and argue, instead, for either pharmacological or prosthetic approaches.

The contrast between the possibilities of amending the body through a combination of determination, lifestyle modification, and surgical intervention and the acknowledgment of progressive physical and mental limitation is striking in the frequent and repeated *Modern Maturity* advertisements for scooters to help those with weakened or disabled legs, especially the ad for Pride Scooters that pictures "Daredevil Legend Evil Knievel On His Legend Scooter" (September/October 2000). Here we see the sixty-three-year-old Knievel, who broke thirty-five bones over eight years of daredevil motorcycle jumps in the 1960s and 1970s and has been valorized in biographical movies, a line of Ideal Toys, and an exhibit in the Smithsonian Institute, sitting on a three-wheeled "Legend" scooter in what amounts to a parodic image of his younger self. Clearly, there is a disjunction between an insistence on the power of the mind and an acknowledgement, through the ads especially, of a real audience whose members have not and cannot overcome their bodies. Given the tendencies of *Modern Maturity* to feature the possibilities for continuing physical, mental, and economic vitality while also including acknowledgments of eventual, inevitable breakdown, the magazine develops a position on abjection that is not unlike that of the aesthetic surgical industry: (1) The abject body is real, and affects the quality of day-to-day life and the possibilities for continuing mobility and social interaction; and (2) abjection can be neutralized if it, like cancer, is "caught early": those who follow the preceptive *Modern Maturity* advice for life management from age fifty onward can continue to resist abjection right through "the good death", but those who are either unlucky or unwise (Knievel's antics represent both) may find themselves past the possibility of resistance and redemption, when all that is left is prosthetics and palliatives. Just so, aesthetic surgical procedures we know are being marketed to ever younger persons, so that teens are now receiving breast and nose jobs for their sixteenth birthdays or high-school graduations.

The *Modern Maturity* article titled "Lucky Star: The Charmed Life of Paul Newman" typifies the magazine's position. It begins by describing a Newman past help and hope, a stroke victim:

> Paul Newman is slumped in a wheelchair. His head lolls, his jaw is slack, the vivid blue eyes stare vacantly into space. A determined nurse tries gamely to cajole, then sweet-talk, and finally intimidate him to snap out of it. But he is totally unresponsive. We squirm, not really wanting to

watch this. Not Paul Newman. And still it goes on, for a good half-hour more, the guy all but dead. So begins *Where the Money Is*, Newman's latest film, and the image he presents is shocking. (Shah 31)

The abject Newman is displaced, of course, by the transcendent Newman in this film and in so many of his others where, as with Cool Hand Luke falsely broken and reduced to servile groveling, Newman's flashing blue eyes and winning smile define the image that, in the end, stays with us. At age seventy-five, Newman is "trim and his face unlined; only his white hair and gravelly voice bespeak his age" (32). This article that advertises the *Modern Maturity* mantra that "the experience of aging in America isn't what it used to be" is immediately followed by an ad for the osteoarthritic medication Vioxx that begins with the question, "What If How Your Body Feels Wasn't Always The First Thing On Your Mind?" (36). The border between the pieces like "Lucky Star," which are consistent with the magazine's celebratory and preceptive view of aging, and the advertisements that speak to an audience in relatively constant pain and awareness of their body's betrayal is yet another line of separation between the secluded elements of physical order, integrity, and vitality and the abject elements of embodied being: pain, breakdown in psychophysical cooperation among the body's organs and parts (as in the "fantasy" of Newman above), social alienation. It is a border, further, between the younger AARP body that can still entertain resilience as a possibility, and the older AARP body that has reached the point of no return. It is a border, finally, between atavism as a cultural preoccupation and resignation to progressive limitation.

The atavism that maintains the body against the borderland is essentially an identification of an aging body with its imagined ancestor, with a version of itself that corresponds with a mental picture of youth and the viability of continued good health. Thus, "modern maturity" gains an influential cultural definition, through the broad distribution of *Modern Maturity* in the United States, as the preservation of as much of one's youth as possible for as long as possible. Put another way, it becomes the hallmark of maturity to resist it (or, as in the 1999–2000 television commercials for L'Oreal cosmetics, "defy it"). Growing old, as an act of solidarity with the marginalized and disabled other, is inconsistent with growing up, which has come to mean exercising the active choice of management techniques and attitudes that promise the continuous improvement of mind and body. Thus, the borders between maturity and aging, the proper body and the abject body, are maintained, and fortified not only in self-help precepts, but also in the medical corollary to the contemporary self-help movement, the aesthetic clinic.[16]

Conclusion

Through many venues—trade books, advertisements, reality television, web pages, talk shows, magazines—the aesthetic surgical imaginary (which is now so pervasive that it may inform all media all the time) has created responses to the charges voiced by second-wave feminism that commercialized beauty objectifies and commodifies the body. This is accomplished, as we see in examples such as *A Personal Story*, the *Oprah Winfrey Show*, and *Modern Maturity*, by stressing the amending of the abject body as a demonstration of agency and autonomy, rather than an act of identification with norms and status that could be understood as subservient conformity. My purpose in stressing the irony of an enthusiasm for autonomy that has become routine justification for a makeover, is not to deny that aesthetic patients are thoughtful agents; rather, I would press the conclusion that the makeover culture of the early twenty-first century is (1) actively complicit with the imaginary that objectifies abject bodies and (2) engaged in the objectification, abjection, and amendment of the body as a means of both coping with death and dissolution and creating the comfort of a validated community.

The recent surge in the performance of aesthetic surgical procedures has provoked social historians, feminist critics, medical practitioners, and laypersons into a vigorous dialogue about the social and cultural significance of the industry. Some see surgical beautifying as an advance in individual freedom, an indication of posthuman possibilities for identity and community, and a cure for feelings of inferiority. Others fear increased intolerance of physical difference, further entrenchment of conventional and oppressive beauty ideals, and the exclusion of low-income individuals from the psychological and health benefits that aesthetic surgery can offer. As aesthetic surgery becomes more fully accepted as a legitimate branch of medicine, questions continue about whether it is committed to healing or to profit making; whether the increase in aesthetic surgical patients corresponds with increased exposure to risky procedures; whether all those who perform aesthetic surgery are medically qualified to do so; and whether the availability of new, better, more affordable procedures will only contribute further to the already large number of persons who see their otherwise healthy bodies as defective.

The nature of beauty is once again a widely debated issue. Elaine Scarry locates the "fluidity" of beauty in its capacity to surprise and enliven, acknowledging the range of perceptual differences that attend the viewing of any object; she claims that beauty moves us to justice by intensifying our interest in fixing the wrongs in the world that the experience of beauty makes that much more intolerable (*On Beauty and Being Just*). Less reverent than Scarry, Eleanor Heartney says, "Beauty seems in need of rehabilitation today as an impulse that can be as liberating as it has been deemed enslaving," and proposes that we "loosen beauty's—or anti-beauty's—attachment to the good and the true" (xiv). Such a statement worries that epistemological and idealizing approaches to beauty (e.g., Soderholm) may not contribute much to understanding its everyday operation as a valuative term for human worth, and complements considerations of how medical constructions of beauty affect cultural difference and emotional pain (e.g., Parens, *Enhancing Human Traits*). Focusing on the ethics of surgical beautifying, Margaret Olivia Little advances a case-specific theory of beauty in which she asks when medicine is responding justly to the pain enforced through socially enforced beauty norms, by giving the patient an appearance less susceptible to ostracism; and when medicine is complicit in the validation of norms that are morally problematic. Medicine's charge is "having compassion for the patients' suffering and alleviating it where possible," but at the same time it must account for "the relation between the surgeon, or indeed medicine as an institution, and the suspect norms and practices themselves" (168–69). She concludes:

> The only way to participate in the surgeries without de facto promoting the evil whose effects one decries is to locate the surgery in a broader context of naming and rejecting the evil norms. One's purpose and meaning—that of alleviating the extreme burdens the system places on some—can be expressed only if one's broader actions stand squarely against the norms. . . . Medicine can take proactive steps to counteract this constriction [of women's self-understanding] by responsibly underscoring the option not to pursue surgery. (173–75)

The ethics of aesthetic medicine rest in this view on the position that resistance to social beauty norms should be one of the options that the industry sells; interpellation by the aesthetic surgical imaginary might then consist of a "Hey, you there" accompanied by a menu of options that does not include body loathing.

The destructive consequences of bracketing away the variant body from our lexicon of personal choices occupies Gail Weiss's reading of Kristevan abjection, in which she asks, "If . . . the construction of the abject other ultimately represents our (unsuccessful) attempts to repudiate our own abjection, what effects do these attempts and the existence of this abject other have upon our own body images and upon our own understanding of the phenomenon of distortion?" (96). The concept of abjection allows us to conclude that the body is maintained in contradiction, in "the irresolvable gap between our own diverse and fluid bodily sensations on the one hand, and our identification with the unified, integrated specular image which subjectivates us" (100). It is the neurotic or psychotic effort to close this gap that produces the hyperdisciplined and destructive body of the anorexic, a body that we mistakenly view as contradictory when it is in fact in active denial of contradiction. We need a new lexicon to talk about the distorted body, one that acknowledges that the "impure chaos" (Grosz) of the subject is "normal," and that what we sometimes understand—as we maintain desire for the coherent body—as "abjection" can instead be understood as a variant body image that coexists with other variants, and allows us to understand the body as a collocation of body images that are inconsistent with one another.

In his study of the goals of medicine, Eric Cassell argues that the surgeon needs to develop an aesthetic sensibility that informs his skill with creating "pleasing" incisions that heal properly (204), and which understands the disharmonies within and upon the individual body as replicated in unfortunate social conditions:

> Look around the areas of your town or city where the comfortable live and notice the concord. In contrast, the slums are usually not only dirty, but disorderly. The walls of this or that building are splashed with graffiti, garbage abounds, there sits an old car on flattened tires or with broken windows. Oases of prettiness or neatness are in contrast with the general untidiness. . . . It should not be surprising, therefore, that just as the poor carry a greater burden of disease and greater family and group strife than the comfortable, so their environment reflects their difficulties. We humans are of a piece; what afflicts a part, afflicts the whole, what disorders the whole disorders the parts. (211)

Here, Cassell identifies the reconciliation of the whole with the disruptive presence of the other, and analogizes the cleanup of social disorder and waste with the curative treatment of the individual body.

Debates over the ethics of aesthetic surgery, focused as they are on the patient's agency as a crucial element, all agree that women's power lies in the capacity for choice and refusal within a complex of difficult and unstable material conditions. The critical analysis of the beauty clinic's oppression, stressing that the clinic offers false choices, may lead us to a less subjugated sense of options for our bodies and allow us to choose modes of resistance freer from compromise with commercial interests. At the same time such resistance is a good, we should not underestimate the difficulty of creating realities free from the desire for some forms of corporeal transcendence. As Frederic Jameson has pointed out, this desire, which he associates with escape from the temporal, is foundational to culture building, leading to the creation of philosophies, histories, politics, art, and aesthetics that aim to transcend time. Kristeva's parallel point is that abjection motivates and maintains the institutions and discourses that seek to repress and eradicate it, so that its specter is foundational to both the psyche and its cultural constructions. If the appeal of the beauty industry seems insuperable, it is because it so directly addresses the problem of this specter, interpellating the human core of physical pain and habituated desire.[1]

One response to our social abjection is strategic conformity of the sort that Kathy Davis allows as a practical alternative to radical resistance for many women, and that other advocates of female empowerment feature in crasser terms as a "dress-for-success" approach. Another response, the one most fully capable of a complex vision of variant bodies and involved in the creative desire to both escape and describe the temporal and corporeal is the consciousness of what I will call "inspired abjection." Inspiration in this concept is founded on materiality and cannot be held exclusive by a patriarchal philosophical aesthetic that celebrates the capacity of the male intellect to soar above common existence. Inspired abjection is performed in the lifting of its contents out of hiding, as with the 1993 Whitney Museum exhibition of "Abject Art" works by Robert Mapplethorpe, Kiki Smith, and Andy Warhol, among others, which featured depictions of disease, waste, dismemberment, and fragmentation in the spectacularization of the ordinary (Houser; see also, e.g., Riddell; Wilson).

This is not to say that abject art is an emergent reconstitution of beauty, or to participate in the "everybody's-beautiful-in-their-own-way" syndrome. There is no gain in wrenching beauty so that it includes wrinkles and spider veins. At the same time that inspired abjection removes all disguise from the abject body, it also acknowledges that conventional valuations of beauty, represented by the aesthetic surgical imaginary, do tend to prevail: for the moment, characteristics such as symmetry, whiteness, and youth are entailed by beauty, and insistence that it might be or should be otherwise will not change that. What inspired abjection may license is the recognition that fetishizing the elements of beauty corresponds with a severely limited understanding of human functionality, versatility, capacity, and both interbodily and intrabodily diversity. Wrinkles are not beautiful, but they are the markers of a sensate and emotional history that can be appreciated as an existential process of momentous events. Understanding the tyranny of the normal[2] as a force that affects the full range of abject bodies—"deformed" by gender ambiguity, race, ethnicity, fat, age, disproportion, disfunctionality, disease—acts of inspired abjection do not deny our desire to lead abjection-free lives; rather, they present conjunctions of the extraordinary and the ordinary. A memorialization of feces as art, for instance, makes abjection part of a process that is aesthetically valuable, as an intensified representation of the sheer elements of being, without responsibility to beauty, or even to distinguishing the normal from the abnormal.[3]

For versions of inspired abjection that are less shocking and more complex than the pile of feces that we get from a Mapplethorpe, we can look, as Donna Haraway has done in her website Modest_Witness@Second_ Millenium, to Lynn Randolph's paintings of women whose bodies that are at once surreal, ordinary, and abject. *Immeasurable Results*, for instance, pictures a woman draped on an MRI table, caught in the articulation of "high-technology capital, diverse skills, interdisciplinary negotiations, bodily organic structures, marketing strategies, personal and public symbolic codes, medical doctrines, transnational economies, scientific industry's labor systems, and patient-consumer hopes and fears" (xiii). Other paintings show women of different ages, ethnicities, shapes and sizes floating in a symbol-laden space-time, about which Randolph says:

> Perhaps by placing women's reality into an SF world, a place composed of interference patterns, contemporary women might emerge as something other than the sacred image of the same, something inappropriate, deluded, unfitting, and magical—something that might make a difference. I believe that we need to be active about this, not removed . . . real (not natural) and soiled by the messiness of life. (273)

We recognize the inspired abject in all superimpositions of the aerobatic and the grounded, conjunctions that disrupt the normal by re-presenting the ordinary as "heterogeneous, strange, polychromatic, ragged, conflictual, incomplete, in motion, and at risk" (Russo vii). Yaeger's sublime "mother" seeks an "appropriate aggression" (16), one that abandons the reproductive woman of the masculinist imagination (who is mute, passive, and prostrate), but does not abandon her own body. Yaeger thinks, in paradoxical terms, that women should not try to transcend their bodies through emphasis on the sublime, but instead access the sublime through bodies that bespeak limitation and trial. The maternal sublime is a communal poetic—dividing itself from a past sublime that valued rugged individualism in favor rather of solidarity among women, and among humanity. The "language of blood" is an aesthetic recognizing that actual childbirth is not necessarily a euphoric experience for all women at all times, that birthing women do experience agony and tragedy, that some do not welcome their pregnancies, and that modern technologies oftentimes rob women of some experiential aspects of giving birth. It is a language admitting that all women are defined, in cultural terms, as potentially grotesque in body; and all persons, to the extent that they are mortal, are tied up with cycles of birth and death. It is a language that informs the lexicon of inspired abjection, as part of the forceful presentation of a complex vision of the persons with variant bodies who both look beyond themselves and find value in their situatedness.[4] It is a language that does not contradict the desire for beauty, or condemn those who display it (as we all do, at one time or another, in one way or another); rather, the language of blood, as another dimension of inspired abjection, keeps beauty in its place.

Robert Frost's "Provide, Provide" recounts the abjection of Abishag, a former Hollywood starlet who becomes a "withered hag." She is not the victim of a magic curse, just aging and the alienation that attends it. It would seem that Abishag's fate surprised her, for it prompts the narrator to warn readers of their similar destiny, and to array the pursuits they might try in order to avoid it: wisdom, virtue, wealth, power, fame, or, taking the shortest route, suicide. But in any case, he admits, nothing "keeps the end from being hard." At best there is the possibility of maintaining a certain social dignity by getting rich enough to afford "boughten friendship": though wisdom and virtue may be worth trying, only wealth and power can keep some admirers around while you decay. You will wither and die, but if your buying power is intact, "nobody can call *you* crone."

The poem responds to a hopeless question—Where is the provision for my abjection?[5]—with advice that is, by turns, benevolent, cynical, and worthless. What does not dissolve into irony is the repeated imperative, "Provide, provide," which is in this case primarily addressed to women doomed to suffer alienation through the loss of beauty. Any narrative compassion, then, is qualified by a certain measure of invulnerability: the narrator here is the crone's advisor, perhaps even a supplicant for her boughten friendship, but does not share her gendered fate. Young, beautiful women are, like the Abishag who entertained the aging King David and provided the name for Frost's crone, called into the service of older men, but left alone and abject in their own old age. Frost at once indicates the urgency of providing for abjection and accords his narrator mock salvific status that is both wry and patriarchal. The aesthetic surgical imaginary also advises us to provide for the abject body. While it enacts the masculinist benevolence that occupies Frost and, more overtly, many of the Romantic writers who mourn lost female beauty (for example, Shelley, Poe, Hawthorne), the aesthetic imaginary trades on neither ambiguity nor irony.

Such motives carry, then, equal measures of necessity and impossibility: we must provide for our abjection, even as we cannot. It is clear to me not only that we need to be provided for in the face of our body's abjection, but also that the looking beyond in which we engage is often problematic: caught in dualistic and hierarchical paradigms that devalue the body, and thus productive of forms of abjection that do not need to exist. We should continue to ask, then, whether the aesthetic surgical industry is providing the right remedy for our abjection, and if we deem not, then ask what the alternatives might be. Until we provide for the abject body in some set of ways better than current medical models of the value of surgical aesthetic transformation, the aesthetic surgical clinic is where people will continue to go for help—and in ever greater numbers.

Jean Baudrillard finds no alternatives to the cultural "surgery of otherness" emblematized by plastic surgery: "There is [no solution] to this erotic movement of an entire culture, none to such a fascination, to such an abyss of denial of the other, of denial of strangeness and negativity." He does, however, imagine the possibility of an "Eros of resistance" replacing this surgical imaginary:

> We can only remember that seduction lies in not reconciling with the Other and in salvaging the strangeness of the Other. We must not be reconciled with our own bodies or with our selves. We must not be reconciled with the Other. We must not be reconciled with nature. We must not be reconciled with femininity (and that goes for women too). The secret to a strange attraction lies here.

The reconciliation against which Baudrillard warns is the philosophical ground for the development of medical aesthetics (a term increasingly used to refer to cosmetic surgery).[6]

When the responsibilities of medical aesthetics to the variant body are better theorized so as to articulate the physical, psychological, social, political, and cultural elements of the struggle between beauty and abjection, perhaps we can begin to "liberate" the aesthetic surgical imaginary from its premises. This is properly a humanistic project, because the central term for investigation—beauty—is at once the most totalized, unstable, and multivalent concept in Western intellectual history and the sensory and intellectual basis for our understanding and validation of humanity. Perhaps alertness to the dynamics of abjection can keep us in this optimistic space, at once within a situated awareness of the problems and limitations—physical, psychological, and social—that prevail with respect to our relationship to our bodies, and alert to the social body's influence on our valuation of appearance. Abjection accounts for the awareness that we do labor under decided material exigencies and constraints, at the same time as it licenses images of the cultural and personal body that are more plastic and fluid and variable than the aesthetic surgical imaginary has allowed. The breakdown of the integrated subject can make possible a solidarity in difference, in the collective recognition of the distinctions and ambiguities of our bodies, and the collective admission of tendencies to abject the other whose body serves as a comforting repository of our fears.[7] It may be that a damaging conformity exists less in acts of beautifying than in the inability to live (in contradiction) with the variant body. If there exists some meeting ground between, or third term beyond, the practice of social and cultural community and the possibilities for living with each other's impurities, it will be sighted through abjection, which accounts for the presentation of the physical self to the social body. Perhaps, in an extraordinary partnership with abjection, which is essentially poetic in its impetus and power, medicine can help to heal cultural representation.

Notes

Introduction

Material on Burke, Kant, and Plato in the section "Objectification and False Consciousness" is adapted from Covino, "Abject Criticism."

1. In *Cosmetic Surgery: The Cutting Edge of Commercial Medicine in America*, Deborah Sullivan studies the growth of the aesthetic surgical industry from a sociological perspective, probing the complicity among technological progress, the commercialization of medicine, and changes in the social status of women. She focuses on industry-sanctioned discussions of aesthetic surgery in women's magazines, and how this discourse has affected acceptance and demand. For Sullivan, the current popularity of aesthetic surgery results from "cultural pressures to be attractive" as well as from aggressive efforts by physicians to extend its scope in light of the Federal Trade Commission's decision to allow medical practitioners to advertise their services to the public. Sullivan is explicit about not wishing to offer a psychological explanation, much less an explanation grounded in philosophical psychology—culturally elaborated—as the nexus of desire; at the same time she identifies "our ideas about appearance" (201) as primary villains in the story of the industry's continuing growth.

2. The identification of good medicine with the transcendence of corporeal limits was aggressively exploited by Nuveen Investments in an advertisement that aired during the 2000 Super Bowl telecast featuring a computer-generated image of actor Christopher Reeve, who suffered paralyzing spinal cord damage in 1995, standing up and walking (Associated

Press, "Ad of Reeve Walking"). The spot calls for financial investment in a future when good medicine (identified by Reeve as "money and talent") produces the amendable, perfectible body. The prospect at once purifies and commodifies the body.

3. By September 2002 the bronze figure and associated procedure lists were replaced by a much more extensive list of procedures and the page was renamed <Ienhance.com>. The name change both avoids confusion with cosmeticsurgery.org, the web page sponsored by the American Academy of Cosmetic Surgeons, and reflects the marketing of a broader range of procedures, including cosmetic dentistry. Advertised surgeons are identified as "I Enhance" doctors and patients are associated with "I Enhance" bodies. This brand-naming of the aestheticized body, coincident with several episodes of testimony by patients about the body parts they can't stand and the procedures they must have, continues the twin themes of body-as-commodity and body loathing that the 2000 version of the web page introduced.

4. Treatments of the subject include Agonito, Covino, de Beauvoir, Dinnerstein, Irigaray, and Suleiman.

5. Especially *Cratylus, Gorgias, Phaedo, Phaedrus, Philebus, Republic,* and *Symposium.*

6. See, for example, "Eyelid Surgery," "Forehead Lift," and "Rediscover the Beauty in Your Eyes."

7. Faludi cites a study done by the Kinsey Institute which showed that American women's hatred of their own bodies is higher than in most other cultures.

8. Susan Sontag's *Illness as Metaphor* makes the case that the thinness ideal is a throwback to the Victorian period in which the tubercular patient was romanticized as a figure of beautiful illness: "Twentieth-century women's fashions (with their cult of thinness) are the last stronghold of the metaphors associated with the romanticizing of TB in the late eighteenth and early nineteenth centuries" (29). Sontag says that many of the literary and erotic attitudes known as 'romantic agony' derive from tuberculosis and its "transformations through metaphor": to be a poet is to be vulnerable, sensitive, suffering, sad, melancholic, even slightly insane (29).

9. Faludi ends her discussion of aesthetic surgery by discussing "Diana Doe," who became anxious after seeing a *Newsweek* cover story declaring that unmarried women in their thirties have a less than 5% chance of ever getting married. (Faludi debunks this as a myth in the early part of the book, along with three other myths calculated to keep women concerned about their situations: that there is a devastating plunge in economic status for woman who divorce under no-fault laws, that there is an infertility epi-

demic among professional women, and that professional women are simply burned out from having to do too much and are not really gratified in their work.) Diana Doe has an exchange with a male reporter and winds up betting him about $1,000 that she will be married by age forty. Doe is fixated on the idea that all that stands in the way of matrimony are certain physical deficits that aging has produced in her. In a chilling moment, she consults a modeling expert who tells her that she should "divide [her] body up into parts and go over each part with a magnifying glass," then cover up what she can't fix and improve the rest (222–26). Diana commits to a full-scale body overhaul in collaboration with a marketing professor who agrees to sell her story to the media for a share of any profits that result. She gets breast implants, trying to quell her fears about the surgery by telling herself that beauty is essential. She is criticized by callers on a radio show, rejected by a potential suitor who thinks she looks too old, and anticipates liposuction as she struggles to lose weight through curbing her diet and weight training. Doe becomes for Faludi a representative victim of the harsh beauty standards of the 1980s.

10. Cosmetic surgery was a 300 million dollar industry at the time of Wolf's writing, having grown, she notes, at a rate of 10% per year (232).

11. Wolf tells us that as surgeons become wealthier and wealthier, they are able to buy more and more advertising space and to exert pressure on the media to do positive stories on the industry.

12. The beauty industry that Wolf and Faludi attack is seen to play into the Freudian suggestion that women's psyches are structured by masochism:

> Since women should suffer to be beautiful—since our suffering *is* beautiful—the pain we feel is "discomfort." Because women's money is not real money but pin money, and because women are fools for "beauty" and a fool and her money are soon parted, fraudulent practices are not fraud and women's play money is fair game. Because women are deformed to begin with, we cannot really suffer deformation. (Faludi 254)

13. Focusing not on technological but cultural practice, Nawal El Saadawi makes an even more radical argument about the lack of choice, comparing aesthetic surgical cutting to "female genital circumcision" in which some young girls in African and Arab countries are mutilated under conditions of torture.

14. Davis's characterization of feminists on the beauty question is somewhat reductive. She generalizes that feminist criticism has typically

condemned women who participate in the beauty system as the victims of false consciousness, as a general castigation that probably calls to mind commentators such as Faludi, Wolf, and Morgan, but which does not specify any particular feminist culprits. Of course, the general spirit of both popular and academic feminism has never been to expose and condemn women, but to speak in objection to the cultural discourses and practices that seek to cripple in all women forms of truly liberating agency. It could be construed as noble to protect women from the harsh scrutinizing light she imagines feminism to shine on their bad decisions; however, it is also a way of constructing feminism in a disparaging way. Popularizing such disparagement, Kimberly Henry and Penny Heckaman's *Plastic Surgery Sourcebook* identifies not only guilt (at defying someone who has recommended against surgery) and vanity among the "inner tyrants" that "hold us back from doing what we want to do" with respect to beautifying, but also the feminist view, at whose proponents these authors direct a great deal of irritated pity (198–99).

15. Balsamo offers an analysis of the industry that stresses many of the same oppressive elements noted by Faludi, Wolf, and Morgan but comes to a rather abrupt conclusion congenial to Davis, that "we may need to adopt a perspective on the bodily performance of gender identity that is not so dogged by neoromantic wistfulness about the natural, unmarked body" (79).

16. Citing Foucault here and below as one who contributes to our understanding of the distribution of power operating within the culture of the aesthetic clinic, I am fully aware that his work has overlooked contributions by women to the understanding of disciplinary power's effects on the body. At the same time, his cultural analysis of power does converge at several points with feminist concerns (see, for example, Diamond and Quinby).

17. Because Davis interviews women in the Netherlands rather than in the United States, there may be cultural differences associated with her results. Davis's methodology involves extensive biographical interviews with ten women, and a clinical study that focused on breast augmentation (thirty accomplished, twelve in process) for white working-class to lower-middle-income women.

18. A number of the women that Davis interviews feel that some part of their body is noticeably abnormal. Davis admits that their perceptions about this are largely incorrect, but argues that unhappiness with one's body is nonetheless a legitimate malady.

19. Gilman, in *Making the Body Beautiful*, applauds Davis's study as the best that feminism has to offer on the subject of surgical beautifying, though he argues that aesthetic surgery is a phenomenon that is far from being limited to women. He writes, "the end of the story is the sense of happiness attributed to the gendered body, whether male or female," and notes "the problem of the

unhappy body image . . . reflects a Western preoccupation with all 'deviant' forms of the body" (xi), including features that betray aging and ethnicity. Thus, Kathy Davis and Sander Gilman reach, from different sets of observations, conclusions that are congenial to one another and indicate that the radicality that characterizes statements by Wolf, Faludi, Bordo, and Morgan may be giving way to a recognition that the aesthetic clinic is here to stay.

20. The states with the highest incidence of aesthetic surgery procedures are, in rank order, California, New York, Florida, and Texas, with Florida ranked number one in per capita procedures.

21. The cultural imaginary that emerges through the work of Lacan, Kristeva, and Althusser can be generalized as an articulated totality of practices and institutions within which people can have agency, but do not "make" the world (Hall).

Chapter 1: Abjection

1. Kristeva's view that body contents are abject because they compromise our maintenance of a clean separation between life and death is supported by Mary Douglas's influential anthropological study *Purity and Danger*, which demonstrates that abjects are inveighed against because they disturb preestablished classification systems.

2. James Joyce is probably the most influential writer on the world stage to be associated by Kristeva with the sort of writing that violates and resists all attempts to impose a stable understanding or interpretation, but is at the same time playful and engaging and musical. As Kristeva says in a 1985 interview with Margaret Smaller, "It is impossible to read [Joyce's] *Finnegan's Wake* without entering into the intrapsychic logic and dynamics of . . . the play of form [and contents]—which is . . . a play of psychic pluralization" (O'Donnell 282). Many critics also cite *Ulysses's* Molly Bloom who, in the novel's final pages, speaks her bodily drives in a way that is revolutionary both for its violation of the proper rules of grammar and for its content. Here is Molly:

> I suppose that what a woman is supposed to be there for or He wouldn't have made us the way He did so attractive to men then if he wants to kiss my bottom Ill drag open my drawers and bulge it right out in his face as large as life he can stick his tongue 7 miles up my hole as hes there my brown part then I'll tell him what I want. . . . (642)

Semiotic language resists the stabilizations of language imposed by the Symbolic Order and rescues the symbolic from becoming *doxic*, or doctrinaire. This is not to say, however, that symbolic ordering is somehow antithetical or hostile to being. Quite the contrary, since Kristeva recognizes the necessary initiation of the subject into language and observes that the alternative to membership in the ordered symbolic is perversion, as she tells us in *Revolution* ("[W]hat distinguishes the poetic function from the fetishist mechanism is that it maintains a *signification*" [115]), and in *Powers of Horror* ("[T]he writer is a phobic who succeeds in metaphorizing to keep from being frightened to death; instead, he comes to life again in signs" [38]).

3. Note the difference between the Symbolic Order and symbolic language: we are all language users—and the symbolic can simply mean signification, which, Kristeva tells us, qualifying Lacan, was already taking place in the semiotic—but our uses of language can be more or less compatible with the Symbolic Order, the rule of law: in Lacan's terms, the Law of the Father.

4. This is one among several of Kristeva's qualifications of Lacan; a calling into question of his idea that entry into the symbolic is a radical, decisive break with what came before (with the Imaginary, in Lacan: unity with the mother and the world). Lacan likes to say that the subject is divided from himself through language. Kristeva returns us to ourselves, to our bodies, when she proposes here that the slide between the semiotic and the symbolic in children's thetic phase of language acquisition is reproduced in poetic language.

5. That such significances for the maternal body are given play in horror movies is evident in the *Alien* series, about creatures that use human bodies as a kind of gestational space before they destructively burst out of their hosts' bodies, killing them. These creatures are figures of the archaic mother, since their activity relative to humans is entirely tied up with the reproductive function, and they have no moral purpose apart from this instinct. Andrea Kuhn has observed that because the alien mother in the series "concentrates solely on her reproductive function and is posited *outside* morality and the law, she threatens the patriarchal symbolic order and has to be negated."

6. Roselyne Rey proposes that perhaps pain can be considered more strictly "physical," and suffering "moral," but adds, "The word suffering seems more to refer to the subject while pain seems more the objectification of this suffering" (3). Elizabeth Spelman makes suffering a central element of the human condition and argues that there are certain benefits of that condition that derive from taking suffering seriously, recognizing that the nature of suffering is not universal, and drawing lessons from the suffering of one group that may be applicable to another. A politics of shared suffering, which her study advances, may be comparable to a politics of shared abjection; however, "abjection" is finally a more powerful term, whose embrace is more difficult and daunting, since it involves regarding a materiality that is revolting and disgusting.

7. Scarry argues that one's own physical pain and the physical pain of others are two wholly distinct orders of events, that our own pain is so unnegotiably present that it may be the primary model of what it means "to have certainty," while the pain of others is so remote and intangible that it may be the primary model of what it means "to have doubt" (4). While we feel our own pain, we can only hear about the pain of others. Scarry proposes that pain is elusive for nonsufferers because it is actually difficult to represent in language: "[P]hysical pain—unlike any other state of consciousness—has no referential content. It is not *of* or *for* anything. It is precisely because it takes no object that it, more than any other phenomenon, resists objectification in language" (5). Scarry points out that psychic suffering has referential content: we feel anguish about something. By contrast, we can only try to represent physical pain by calling upon damage (injury) and agency (weapon) as testimony, but finally, communicating the reality of pain to people who are themselves not in pain is a difficult task. Because pain destroys the contents of consciousness (one can think of nothing but the pain), pain is the deconstruction of the self. Without a public voice (Bakan 64), and present nowhere "on the visible surface of the earth" (Scarry 3), pain belongs wholly to interior experience, so that woe, words, and world form a nexus of lonely meaning for the suffer.

Byron Good discusses a four-hour conversation with a young man suffering from chronic pain, whose own language breaks down as he tries to describe his condition (29–48). The speechlessness of pain was recognized as early as the second century CE by Galen, who said that "it is evidently impossible to transmit the impression of pain by teaching, since it is only known to those who have experienced it. Moreover, we are ignorant of each type of pain before we have felt it" (Siegel 190). Sherwin Nuland observes that physicians and nurses underestimate the degree of pain suffered by the ill, primarily because comprehending the magnitude of pain that accompanies medical conditions is very difficult for those who have not experienced it ("A Munch Moment: 'The Scream' or 'The Whimper'").

8. Alfred Adler's concept of the "inferiority complex" opened the way (Haiken 111–18).

9. Sabbath and Hall write at length in *End Product: The First Taboo* that the vagina has often been thought of as a kind of toilet or waste container for men's sperm.

10. The discussion of Yaeger and Russo below is adapted from Covino, "Abject Criticism."

11. She discusses Mary Oliver's poem "Strawberry Moon" in this context: Elizabeth Fortune, having had a romantic experience with a young man who then abandons her for another woman, retires to the attic, where, it is suggested,

her life simply stops. She has a child by her lover, but the child is whisked away, the blood from the birth washed clean and the sheets burned, as if the birth were a dirty secret. Following this birth, Fortune spends forty years confined to the attic room. Yaeger notes that while Fortune is imprisoned in obscurity, the father of her child goes out into the light of day, to marry, father legitimate children, and work. He may be a common laborer, but at least he is free. Later in Oliver's poem, however, things begin to change: women begin to take on more aggressive postures, they sometimes "want to lash out with a cutting edge" (Yaeger 8). For Yaeger, Oliver's "scrappy women refuse to lie down" (9); they represent a conversion for femininity.

12. This woman, I would add, is the "angel in the house" who became a conventional female type in the nineteenth century and is associated with passivity, invisibility (except when she presents quiet beauty to the world), and invalidism.

13. Throughout this study, I write of the aesthetic surgical patient exclusively as a "she," while I recognize that a number of commentators are calling into question the reduction of discussion about body image and oppression to the lives of women alone. Susan Bordo's *The Male Body* argues that men are now beginning to undergo all of the indignities and cruelties associated with owning flesh exposed to the cultural gaze as sexed; Susan Faludi's *Stiffed* observes that contemporary men, too, have begun to be co-opted by the image-making systems of postmodern commodity media culture. Harrison Pope says that men are susceptible to developing "pathological shame about their bodies" under the influence of male action toys such as G.I. Joe with their unrealistically trim and muscular physiques (Wheeler). Lynne Luciano proposes in *Looking Good* that men are more self conscious than ever about their physical appearance and are beginning to enter the aesthetic clinic in growing numbers.

Sander Gilman and Elizabeth Haiken report numbers suggesting that men will soon make up nearly one third of all aesthetic surgery patients. However, both Haiken and Gilman draw this conclusion based on 1995–96 statistics for facial surgery only, leaving uncertain the percentage of men represented in the full range of aesthetic surgical procedures. It is the case that, apart from a bit of a rise in the early 1990s, the percentage of men electing aesthetic surgery has held steady at roughly 10%, according to both the American Society for Aesthetic Plastic Surgery and the American Society for Plastic Surgeons. Percentages aside, one has to look separately at the significance of aesthetic surgery for each sex, since what surgical choices may say about gender conditioning is a crucial issue. Just as women tend to seek aesthetic surgery in order to fit more closely the figure of male desire, to become more feminine, men are the targets of appeals to maintain "the ideal male body shape," which is "trim and athletic-looking, with broad shoulders and chest, a flat abdomen, and a narrow hip-thigh area" (ASPRS "Plastic Surgery Indications" brochure). Such an appearance can involve calf implants, pectoral implants, and abdominal etching (which creates a muscular, rippled appearance) and coincides with the image of physical strength and dominance that can come from weight lifting. Luciano supports this view, arguing in *Looking Good,* "Looking good is part of a quintessential male strategy whose ultimate aim is to make men more successful, competitive, and powerful. The means of achieving this goal may be new, but the objective is not" (12).

Aesthetic modification of the symptoms of aging draws the lowest percentage of men: only about 5% of those who want wrinkles removed are male. This may be because wrinkles are not a sign of weakness in men and are a strong sign of abjection in women, whose aged bodies are associated with the witch/hag/grotesque. Recalling Benjamin Gelfant, who writes in *Cosmetic Surgery: A Patient's Guide,* that "on the whole, women tend to love men for their character while men tend to love women for their appearance" (10), we can note that wrinkles on a male face are widely regarded as signs of "character," while for women they are defects in appearance.

The focus on women as the nearly exclusive audience for the marketing of aesthetic surgery is particularly striking in Patricia Burgess's *Aesthetic Surgery Without Fear,* where she writes, "Throughout the book we have chosen to use the terms 'he,' 'him,' and 'his' when referring to physicians and 'she,' 'her,' and 'hers' when referring to patients. Our intent is to be clear and less cumbersome with the verbiage in this book, not to be exclusionary" (x). Add to this statement the many instances of advertising that depict woman as the improvable subject of the male surgeon's medical and artistic skills. Thus, I do not think we can erase the history of women's oppression under the beauty ideal with a few selective recent statistics indicating a possible trend toward greater participation on the part of men. We must ask questions about the kinds of liberation each sex imagines—and achieves—through participation, and about the kinds of witting or unwitting bondage each separately implies. Such a view of gender and surgical beautifying is, I think, consistent with Kristeva's positing of the abject mother as a scene of the flesh's displacement onto women. In this regard, Francette Pacteau theorizes the appeal of beauty as the male's desire to repossess the skin, and reinhabit the body of the mother.

Though Luciano does not view men's entry into the aesthetic surgical clinic as a feminizing act, I would nonetheless want to express the hope that if indeed men are beginning to come to the clinic in greater numbers, possibilities for men's solidarity with women on the beauty front will emerge. If there are signs of a real shift in male awareness of body oppression, perhaps it can allow for a coalition between men and women with regard to the pressures that we be always beautifying ourselves. If so, there may be opportunity for feminists to invite men into an understanding of what it is to have one's flesh objectified, scrutinized, and commodified. This is a possibility that we want to remark, and not neglect.

Chapter 2: Normalizing the Body

1. The abject body really must be kept in check, of course: Kristeva observes that the alternative to membership in the symbolic order is perversion (*Revolution* 115) or psychosis (*Powers* 38). Accession to life and subjecthood comes through violent sublimation against the desublimated void: "'I' am in the process of becoming an other at the expense of my own death. During that course in which 'I' become, I give birth to myself amid the violence of sobs, of vomit" (*Powers* 3). Abjection is dispersed through the production and sloughing off of death's objects: sobs and vomit contest their own repulsive status as the body abjects them in defiance of the objectlessness and subjectlessness that is abyss. However, there is in the transcendent motive the horror of "perfect sublimation," in which the unruly body is suppressed and denied by systems that revile their abjects.

2. Over the last three decades, we have learned a great deal about the Western tradition's suppression of the body. Michel Foucault, Julia Kristeva, Jacques Lacan, Mark Johnson, Leo Bersani, Caroline Walker Bynum, Michel Feher, Michael Camille, Thomas Laqueur, Peter Brown, Susan Suleiman, and Jane Gallop, among many others, have shown repeatedly that discourses of the body, whether philosophic, religious, civic, medical, or scientific, have often had as their primary function austere control of the body—against its needs and pleasures. Foucault's work especially reinforces the idea that structures of power maintain their hold on the body through language, and that language not only serves as a substitute for the body, but also represses certain forms of desire to the extent that it acts to constitute desire itself. The articulation of what is "true" about the body leads to a law of the body that tells people what they can and cannot do with their bodies, what they should and should not desire.

Eve Sedgwick proposes that a subtext guides Foucault's work on sexuality: the body subjected to controlling discourses is one whose desires are specifically homoerotic.

3. Not all the world's scars need to be hidden: some emblematize courage, perseverance, or skill, such as the battle scar, the dueler's scar, and in recent years, the athlete's scar that has been featured in a series of 1999 Nike television commercials that show scarred athletes with determined, sweaty faces, all representing the company motto, "Just Do It." Though the aesthetic sur-

gical scar is still subtended by secrecy rather than celebration, it could soon become a mark of status. ASAPS consumer surveys tell us that a majority of Americans now approve of aesthetic surgery; as we become more forthcoming about our surgeries, perhaps competitive about the quality of our aesthetic surgical scars, we might even find ourselves comparing them to each other's. However, the obsession with either hiding or comparing aesthetic scars is a refusal in both instances to reveal our abjection as such, to present the marks on our bodies as confessions of its mortality.

4. While any number of aesthetic procedures continue to involve pain and scarring, procedures are fast emerging that involve much less of this. We are told repeatedly in advertisements for the clinic's services that procedures are now easier to arrange, less invasive, and subject to constant technological upgrades. Representing the aspiration on the part of surgeons to fully mitigate abjection, Henry and Heckaman write, "The ultimate goal for any plastic surgeon is to perform a face-lift without an incision, perhaps one of these days, but not soon" (66). The laser beam is an especially desirable surgical tool because it performs a "bloodless surgery" (Gelfant 51; Sarnoff and Swirsky 6). The beam ushers in a new era of ease and convenience, in which "Problems that in the past required lengthy medical or surgical treatments—all of them imperfect—are now eradicated in minutes with minimal discomfort and few aftereffects" (Sarnoff and Swirsky 3). See also, for instance, Morris, *The Culture of Pain.*

5. In its 2000 annual advertising insert, "Plastic Surgery Today," published in *USA Today,* the American Society of Plastic Surgeons asks, "Is Plastic Surgery For You? Statistics Say Yes: Ever wondered who's actually having plastic surgery? Look in the mirror. It's not just celebrities and the wealthy who are seeking the services of plastic surgeons. Today's plastic surgery patient encompasses both sexes and touches all age groups, races and economic levels (1). The aesthetic surgical mythos trades widely, inculcating itself into the mirrors of mass culture.

6. Of these top seven procedures, only liposuction is formally termed "surgical" by the ASAPS, that is, involving a cutting through the skin. I do not maintain this surgical/nonsurgical distinction, because (1) the distinction is not held by the professional organizations themselves, through their inclusion of everything from microdermabrasion to abdominoplasty as the practice of aesthetic surgeons; and (2) no current procedure is noninvasive: all involve the injection, incision, removal, dissolution or destruction of some part of the body.

7. The 1955 establishment of the International Confederation for Plastic, Reconstructive, and Aesthetic Surgery gave global presence to aesthetic surgery, especially with the emergence of its most prominent chapter, the

International Society of Aesthetic Plastic Surgery (ISAPS). The ISAPS was constituted in 1970 at the headquarters of the United Nations, a location deliberately chosen to "reaffirm the international scope of the Society" (Hinderer), and occupies a sphere of influence that coincides with that of the Confederation, which includes chapters in eighty-three countries and a membership of 13,500 surgeons worldwide.

8. Sander Gilman proposes that clinical definitions of unhappiness with the body coincident with the developing popularity of rhinoplasty are based in totalitarian theories of race holding Jews to be immutably corrupt in both appearance and character. Some theories argued that even the pronunciation of Yiddish was tied to the way in which the speaker's nose was formed. Gilman cites nineteenth-century physician Bernhard Blechmann, who said that the Jew's "muscles, which are used for speaking and laughing are used inherently differently from those of Christians and that this use can be traced . . . to the great difference in their nose and chin," and thus moved "the 'unhappy' psyche marked by the ugly nose that evokes disease . . . into the world of race and politics" (*Creating Beauty* 74–76). A belief emerges in racial theory that coincides with the motive and justification for aesthetic surgery: inner virtue, or lack of it, corresponds to outward physical features.

This connection is facilitated by Ernst Kretschmer, who posited three body types and associated each with a particular character. His conjunctions were taken up by Ludwig Stern-Piper (much to Kretschmer's chagrin) to correspond to basic racial types. Moses Julius Gutmann also tried to make Kretschmer's constitutional types stand for specific mental illnesses: "The so-called predominance among Jews . . . of the asthenic body type of a long, lanky body suggested to [Gutmann] that they would be particularly subject to schizophrenia, but in his own clinical work he found a predominance of manic-depressive psychosis among Jews" (*Creating Beauty* 79). In other words, Jewish appearance was taken as "scientific evidence of the Jew's inherently pathological condition" (*Creating Beauty* 79). Gilman reports that Jews were associated, in particular, with tuberculosis, since it was thought to attack those with weak constitutions.

9. In a caution against lips that are so racially aberrant as to be dehumanizing, Gelfant comments in passing here that excessive fullness makes women look like Daisy Duck.

10. Jackson's nose, for instance, has been made progressively smaller, so that by 2000 it was not much more than a bump.

11. See, for example, Adams, who arranges his guidebook chronologically, with chapters on "The Twenties," "The Thirties," "The Forties," and so forth, with the proposition that "with the pressures placed on women today, it is no

wonder that many of you are considering procedures at younger and younger ages" (73). Adams reinforces the industry campaign against difference not only by prescribing lifelong aesthetic modification, but also by departing quickly from the implications of his title, *Everything Women of Color Should Know About Cosmetic Surgery*, to a discussion that scarcely acknowledges cultural identity as an element of the patient's decision. Instead, he insists emphatically, without explanation, *"Women of color seeking plastic surgery consultation do not hate themselves and they are not trying to look white"* (4, italics in original).

12. Though there is speculation that Nile-dwellers "used cosmetics to protect their skin from the sun as early as 10,000 [BCE]" (Gaynor 21–22).

13. Note the ironic resemblance of the drinking of hemlock to "prevent excessive breast growth" in the sixteenth century (Engler 6) to today's practice of injecting Botox under the facial skin to paralyze muscles that cause lines and furrows in the skin.

14. The term "beauty doctor" is not Hinderer's, but refers here to the castigatory term that plagued the profession through the first half of the twentieth century; see Haiken 44–90.

15. For Bataille, "Beauty is desired in order that it may be befouled," and befouling is "the essence of eroticism" (144–45). Thus, a woman's beauty is, for Bataille, the essence of her "humanity." This section on beauty in *Erotism* adds up to the opinion that a woman's beauty is a mask for the core ugliness of her genital body and the sex act that this dualistic body inspires.

Chapter 3: Outside-In

1. This authentic, originary self exists in the epistemological frame that distinguishes the natural from the unnatural: by promising that aesthetic surgery can "uncover the natural beauty you thought you lost," a *Palm Beach Post* ad effectively features the wrinkle-free face as natural and the wrinkled one as unnatural, setting a true and beautiful self in opposition to one's exterior deteriorations ("Rediscover the Beauty in Your Eyes"). With this same emphasis on the beauty of the body as natural, Benjamin Gelfant writes, "Wrinkles are usually not the result of natural aging and drying of the skin; they are caused by radiation and chemical damage" (46). Here, the sun, an aspect of the environmental context, is understood as interacting in an unnatural way with the body, despite the fact that the body depends on the sun to live. Gelfant reveals antipathy toward the forces in the environment that affect the body as well as resistance to the body's own inherent tendency to lose beauty. The unnatural muting of the inner self is seen to impose devastating losses on human history by Henry and Heckaman, who add historical

and medical legitimacy to this view by quoting the famous nineteenth-century rhinoplasty surgeon John Orlando Roe: "How much valuable talent had been buried from human eyes, lost to the world and society by reason of embarrassment caused by the conscious, or in some cases, unconscious influence of some physical infirmity or deformity or unsightly blemish" (6).

2. The aesthetic surgeon typically invests himself with considerable power. The initial consultation itself begins to promote psychological happiness, with the surgeon acting as psychoanalyst and counselor, whose job to "relieve anxiety" ("When Choosing a Plastic Surgeon") will leave the patient believing that transformation is already occurring.

3. The deeper inner self imagined here remains relatively unchanging, while the psyche, like the body, is the more mutable.

4. Industry trade books characteristically cite a universal prejudice in favor of good looks, which dictates that attractive people are more likely to get jobs because they are thought to be "more intelligent, more capable," or "warm, sensitive, kind, interesting, poised, and outgoing" (see, for example, Engler 4–5).

5. Brown studies the practices of continence, celibacy, and virginity that developed within Christian populations from 40 to 400 CE (roughly the time of Paul through Augustine) in order to show that sexual abstinence was considered the mark of spiritual closeness to God, a distinction that held out the promise of eternal life. The patristics considered sexual restraint necessary to piety: Irenaeus and Tertullian emphasized the gradual waning of sexual activity within marriage as preparation for union with God; the Desert Fathers, such as Anthony, saw the chastened body as a way to transform the soul, and Augustine idealized all forms of sexual renunciation.

6. The "fear of natural death," which is the traditional province of religious therapies, becomes by 2000 the primary focus of academic science (Sapolsky), with biomedical research in this area drawing a growing proportion of federal funding and senescence—along with allied conditions associated with the disappearance of youth and beauty—becoming "one of science's most glamorous topics" (Horgan). It seems important in such a cultural climate to note and theorize the special significance of a branch of medicine that aestheticizes the body for purported medical purposes.

7. Christian ascetic practices had as their primary function austere control of the body, against its needs and pleasures. Foucault argues that sexuality has not been renounced but remains, instead, an obsessive human concern, as evidenced by the attempts of religion, medicine, philosophy, education, and politics to determine its character, and control its practices. The "repressive hypothesis"—in Freudian terms, that we censor our sexual desires and relegate

them to the subconscious or unconscious—is utterly false; "since the classical age there has been a constant optimization and an increasing valorization of the discourse on sex," and the last three centuries in particular have produced a proliferation of such discourses. The early eighteenth century made sex a "police matter," with its interest in "population" as an economic and political problem. Populations had to maintain a balance between available resources and growth, and sex was at the heart of this effort, making it necessary to analyze the rates of legitimate and illegitimate births, the rate of marriage, the effects of unmarried life, rates of fertility and sterility, frequency and precocity of sexual relations, and so on. Foucault thinks that the ancient and medieval dispositions to subdue the flesh became, by the eighteenth century, a more highly regulated, we might say "technologized" effort that manifests itself in a "polymorphous incitement to discourse" that includes surveillance, regulation of family structure, the classification and medicalization of sexual perversions, and the scientizing of sexuality and the body.

8. The aesthetic surgical imaginary promises to effect the glorified body in life, bypassing the stage of waiting and longing for physical purification as is expressed in Christian doctrine and thought. In *The Saints, When Absent From the Body, Are Present With The Lord* Jonathan Edwards describes the perfection of the body achieved after death, in the sight of God:

> That perfect sight will abolish all remains of deformity, disagreement, and sinful unlikeness; as all darkness is abolished before the full blaze of the sun's meridian light: it is impossible that the least degree of obscurity should remain before such light; so it is impossible the least degree of sin and spiritual deformity should remain, in such a view of the spiritual beauty and glory of Christ, as the saints enjoy in heaven; when they see that Sun of righteousness without a cloud, they themselves shine forth as the sun, and shall be as little suns, without a spot. For then is come the time when Christ presents his saints to himself, in glorious beauty; "not having spot, or wrinkle, or any such thing . . ." (5)

In the bright future of the aesthetic surgical imaginary, the patient may escape the stage of dying that precedes the "perfect rest" time of waiting—already saved—to be reunited with the body; the earthly life will remain the only one, and we will be beautiful in *it*.

9. Like Catherine Gallagher and Thomas Laqueur's *The Making of the Modern Body,* which evidences a growing interest on the part of medical science in taxonomizing and deciphering body parts, Stafford's investigation

into the Enlightenment project to visually probe the body's limits supports Foucault's theory of monopolizing discourses of the body. Foucault would undoubtedly agree that a chilling, detached objectivity must be the result of scientistic discourses of the body, discourses that seek to name its parts and determine its functions and uses, as well as its pathologies.

Chapter 4: "I'm Doing It for Me"

1. Though 1950s situation comedies such as *Father Knows Best* presented an influential but sanitized picture of American family life, we might associate the debut of reality television with the 1973 PBS documentary, *An American Family*, which presented the breakdown of the Loud family in a twelve-hour series culled from three hundred hours of footage. The continuing success of *Candid Camera* from the 1960s forward attests to the appeal of that voyeurism that continues to inform the popularity of today's more spectacular reality shows, such as *Survivor.*

2. Founded by Chairman and CEO John Hendricks, the Discovery Channel was the first product to offered by the Cable Educational Network.

3. Discovery Communications enjoyed revenues of more than 250 million dollars in 2000 (http://www.discovery.com/corporate/finance/revenue.html August 24, 2002).

4. The website tells us that "TLC has continued to set news ratings records in both households and among adults 25–54. According to the 2000 Equitrend Study of brand awareness, TLC ranked second out of 53 television brands for overall quality, behind Discovery. Among fully distributed networks, TLC ranked in the top five in viewer satisfaction, programming quality, importance to the enjoyment of cable, and perceived value among viewers in the Fall 2000 Beta Cable Subscriber Study" (http://tlc.discovery. com August 24, 2002).

5. Though the legitimation of plastic surgery through the first half of the twentieth century largely rested on its reconstructive mission (especially with reference to disfiguring war injuries), over the last fifty years, the aesthetic mission has gained equal importance as a contribution to human health and well-being. Though *A Personal Story* includes reconstructive surgery as a prospective topic and invites interest from reconstructive patients, very few of the programs follow a reconstructive process. The proportion of attention devoted to aesthetic surgery sends the message that altering the body for aesthetic purposes is just as warranted as and much more prevalent than surgery to intervene in abnormality, disease, dysfunction, or impairment.

6. Alan Gaynor, for instance, assures readers that "[t]he improvement in self-esteem, confidence, and outlook can be so great as to last a lifetime" (3–4).

7. Disability studies can contribute to this project, because it is beginning to address the ways in which disability has been tied up with the normalizing of the body and the impossibility, unthinkability, unacceptability, or disallowability of the variant body (Thomson). The movement away from understanding disability exclusively as a clinical condition, toward social constructionist analysis (Linton, Michael Oliver, Thomson), reinforces our focus here on an imaginary that evades its complicity with social engineering. See especially Silvers.

8. Mulvey uses psychoanalysis to reveal the way in which mainstream narrative film is structured by "the unconscious of patriarchal society." She looks at phallocentrism, and its dependence on the castrated woman. Mulvey points out that this power achieved through the phallus is paradoxical in its dependency on the female, on her lack, in order to define itself. The woman is important to the process of phallocentrism in two ways: because she is that against which the phallus defines itself, and because she supports the initiation of the child into the realm of the symbolic. As Mulvey says, her desire is only to capitulate, to serve the desire and power that resides in the phallus. She is "bound by a symbolic order in which man can live out his fantasies and obsessions through linguistic command by imposing them on the silent image of woman still tied to her place as bearer, not maker, of meaning" (439). She argues that cinema, in particular, is "an advanced representation system . . . [that] structures ways of seeing and pleasure in looking" (439). She acknowledges that there are two kinds of cinema, mainstream and alternative. Placing hope in the alternative cinema to give birth to a new aesthetic and politics, Mulvey analyzes the mainstream cinema's "formal preoccupations [which] reflect the psychical obsessions of the society which produced it."

9. By June 2002, fifty episodes of *A Personal Story* had been completed and were cycling through the telecast schedule at the rate of ten per week (two per day); as new episodes were filmed, they were interspersed with reruns. By October 2002, sixty-six programs reviewed for this chapter included "Gabrielle's Lipo," "Tightening Trina's Tummy," "Kathy's Correction," "Phoenix Lift," "Enhancing Amy," "Slimming Down Sarah," "Carrie's Terrific Teeth," "Lighter in Lakeside," "Iidiko's Eyes," "Tyler's Thigh Tuck," "Baby Courtland," "Danielle's Day," "Patrick's Repair," "Removing Sarah's Scar," "Allison's Augmentation," "Thin in San Francisco," "The Smiling Detective," "Lifting Andre," "Arizona Reduction," "Laura's New Nose," "Ana's Aloha Body" (discussed below), "Baby Daria," "Catherine's Courage," "Jill's Bodybuilding Journey," "New Nose, New Life," "Lifting Lisa," "Helping Hashi's Smile," "Facial Rejuvenation," "Leslie's Graduation Nose," "Elvia's New Figure," "A Gift for Kayse," "Sharon's Big City Facelift," "Baby Emma," "Decreasing

Sylvia's Cup," "Jane's Journey Back," "Three Kids and a Tummy Tuck," "Increasing Christi's Cup," "Reconstructing Christine," "Uncovering Debbie's Smile," "Manhattan Power Lipo," "Leveling Laurel," "Marta's Facial Miracle," "Joe's New Do," "Krystal's Tuck," "Devin's Lift," "Bigger in Berkeley," "Linda's Smile," "Contouring Christie," "Windy City Facelift," "Kiki Kicks It Up," "Fatima's Flawless Nose" (discussed below), "Dad's Nose Goes" (discussed below), "Bascari Liposuction," "Angela B in the Cup of C," "Fat Free in New York," "Angela's Abdomen," "Francisco Frank," "Reducing Kelly," "Lori's Getting Larger," "Show Me the Tummy!" "Brandon's New Face," "Light in Jodi's Eyes" (discussed below), "Bigger in Texas," "Saving Kara," "Teenage Transformation," and "Going Sleeveless." By February 2004, *A Personal Story* had suspended production, just as the ABC series *Extreme Makeover* was make aesthetic surgery success stories a weekly feature of prime time network television.

10. Without cosmological fanfare, Barbara Fletcher rejects her father's influence on her features in "Dad's Nose Goes." Of course, any permanent aesthetic change excises part of one's lineage.

Chapter Five: Making Over Abjection

1. *The Chronicle of Higher Education* reports that "Reading Oprah" has become an English course offering at the University of Alberta, where students "explore the many facets of Oprah—race and history; literacy and her book club; self-help and subjectivity" ("U. of Alberta Course Examines Mystique of Oprah Winfrey").

2. Programs discussed or considered in this section include "Millennium Makeovers with Tyra Banks" (January 3, 2000); "High Tech Communications Makeovers" (January 31, 2000); "Weight Loss First" (February 2, 2000); "Gary Zukav on Finding Meaning & Purpose in Your Life" (February 10, 2000); "Take It Off!" (February 11, 2000); "Sela Ward on Ageism in Hollywood" (February 28, 2000); "Age Defying Women" (May 5, 2000); "Lifestyle Makeovers" (May 29, 2000); "Gary Zukav on Fear" (June 5, 2000); "Choose Your Life" (June 21, 2000); "Gary Zukav on How to Get Your Power Back" (January 4, 2001); and "Does This Make Me Look Fat?" (February 23, 2001).

3. There is an ongoing recognition in the makeover arena that normalcy is time-bound and transient, and that tending toward the fashion preferences of one's adult children—in effect taking on the disguise of youth—is preferable to modeling the identity established during one's own youth: "Connie" is applauded for giving up "her big hair" to achieve a new look "that'll take her into 2000 with style," while Justin complains about his mother that she "has had the exact same look year after year after year."

4. Of candidates for "millennium makeovers" Oprah says, "My guests today are wanted. Some of them were even turned in by members of their own family, charged with living in a time warp" (January 3, 2000).

5. Baartman's skeleton and genitalia have been preserved for display in the Musée de l'Homme in Paris.

6. As Rosemary Garland Thomson explains, the spectacle focused on the Hottentot Venus is part of the urgency to maintain a distinctively Caucasian American sense of normalcy, standing for "everything the [emigrated] Englishman considered himself not to be" (71).

7. The first "Lifestyles Makeover" program airs three days after the Morrison discussion (May 29, 2000).

8. Eventually Claudia, too, becomes acculturated, internalizing the aesthetic preferences of the culture in which she lives. If she initially asks, "What made people look at [little white girls] and say, 'Awwwww,' but not for me?" (22), she also says, "I learned much later to worship [Shirley Temple], just as I learned to delight in cleanliness, knowing, even as I learned, that the change was adjustment without improvement" (23). Resistance to the system, however, later motivates Claudia's telling of Pecola's story and informs her perspective on the sad facts of the situation. Pecola is sadly the major victim of racial and colorist prejudice, her own mother treating her rather heartlessly while lavishing affection on the white child in her care, and her own father raping her as a response to his own humiliation by whites.

9. See Susan Willis, "I Shop Therefore I Am: Is There a Place for Afro-American Culture in Commodity Culture?" for further discussion of these connections.

10. These fictional treatments of Barbie correspond to some extent with the actual efforts of Cindy Jackson, now in her late twenties, who has subjected herself to multiple surgical procedures in the quest for a viable Barbie body through two full facelifts, jawline surgery, breast reduction *and* augmentation, and permanent makeup, at a cost of about $100,000.

11. The *Palm Beach Post* ran a story in 1999 that featured an imaginary Barbie at forty who looks more like a sixty-year-old, which is an indication of just how bad the forensic artist, Kendra Mauldin, believes age forty to be for women. Mauldin says that "Barbie's whole body is out of proportion, but her neck really stands out." At the same time as Mauldin seems intent to satirize Barbie's image by making her skin extra coarse from "all that time in the Malibu sun," and the skin above her upper lip extra creased from smoking ("Hey—you might smoke, too, if you had to juggle payments on the Dream House, three or four pink convertibles, a bright yellow helicoptor, and a vast, sequin-studded wardrobe"), the article seems targeted to an aesthetic surgical

culture: a "derma peel" is recommended by Palm Beach dermatologist Layne Nisenbaum for slight forehead wrinkling and collagen injections for thinning lips. Assorted make-up and fashion tips are included to make cheeks look less sunken, eyes less droopy, nose less sharp, and chin and jaw less saggy and heavy. Mauldin comments, "Before I put the hair on her, I was looking at E.T."

12. The Barbie icon's inclusiveness does have limits. Mattel pulled out of production the "Butterfly Art Barbie," which had tattoos, triple-pierced ears, and nose studs, following objections from parents who saw the dolls at a 1998 toy fair. The *Palm Beach Post* reports that in order to remove the modish markings, the dolls were given "plastic surgery," a choice of words whose double meaning should be clear ("Barbie Loses Butterfly Tattoo").

Another recent identification that Mattel seems to have welcomed on the other hand is disability: Duke University Medical Center has used Barbie doll "knees" as finger joints in amputees' prosthetic hands. Barbie's plasticity, it seems, can swing toward both beauty's objects and its rejects ("Barbie's High-Kicking Legs Debut as Prosthetic Fingers").

13. DuCille reveals that the "Shani" line of Barbie dolls, while purported to feature more authentically black body types, maintains the same—or even more petite—proportions of the traditional line, creating the illusion of fuller hips by arching the doll's back (124).

14. Nuland insists that "by and large, dying is a messy business" (142).

15. *The New York Times* reports that 1997 sales of foods and beverages with herbal additives will rise by nearly twenty billion dollars by the end of 2001 (Barnes and Winter, May 28, 2001; 14).

16. 2001 began with another "new look" for *Modern Maturity*, as it introduced a format that is, according to editorial director Hugh Delahanty, "packed with the possibilities of life" (March-April 2001). This *Modern Maturity* features a wider spectrum of shorter articles on health, relationships, and money management, and a new logo—*mm*—printed in large lowercase letters with the full title spelled out in much smaller letters below, along with the elimination of the AARP acronym from the corner of the cover. Thus, *mm* effaces its readers' qualification for receiving the magazine—age-based maturity—at the same time that its distribution is refocused on older AARP members: members aged fifty to fifty-five began in spring 2001 to receive a new magazine, *My Generation*, while those fifty-five and over continued to receive *mm*. The lead feature of this new *mm* for older readers is "Cosmetic Surgery: Is It For You?" a largely commendatory survey of attitudes, experiences, and information in support of the very positive acknowledgment that a large segment of *mm* readership—those fifty-five to sixty-four—is the group

that accounts for much of the increase in aesthetic surgery procedures. This issue concludes, "We have seen the future of cosmetic surgery—and it is us" (Grant 56).

In March 2003, all AARP members began to receive *AARP: The Magazine*, which reintegrated the target audiences for *mm* and *My Generation*, with the declaration by Editor Hugh Delahanty that "what unites the generations is much more powerful than what separates us—particularly in the aftermath of 9/11. Intergenerational harmony is the future" (6).

Conclusion

1. Recent attempts to theorize beauty (e.g., Kirwan, Pacteau, Rorty, Scarry, Soderholm) indicate the general and rather wide-ranging recognition of the continuing power of its appeal and curiosity about what it is. Focusing on the objectification of women, Pacteau acknowledges that the sign of the beautiful can be dehumanizing, while she wonders why the desire for beauty continues to be so strong, a question that has become even more difficult to the extent that the nature of beauty has been so fully ambiguated and its primacy so fully contested. It remains to be seen whether this more general body of work can supply a theory of beauty that does not bracket away abjection and which resonates in reconsiderations of praxis by the medical and beauty industries that let go of neoclassical and enlightenment epistemologies of the beautiful.

2. I borrow from the title of Leslie Fiedler's book, which focuses on the constructedness of abnormality.

3. Because the abject body confuses the distinction among what we contain, produce, and expel, Martin Jay has discussed abjection as a concept that brings the possibility and practice of polis-oriented integrity under scrutiny and that impugns any form of group behavior in which "integrity is bought at the necessary cost of excluding others" (235). He explains that solidarity is necessary to political action and abjection not only denies the stability and solidity of the body that maintains its integrity and knows its boundaries, but also opposes the solidarity of an activist community. The person steeped in abjection, because she has no stable or delimited identity, is also necessarily apolitical, unable to take action against "the powers of horror, powers whose reach extends well beyond the covers of a novel or the walls of a museum" (247). Abject politics, then, is an oxymoron, because the subjecthood and solidarity needed for a politics is devastated by abjection's dissolution of identity.

If abject politics is oxymoronic, so is abject art. Referring to an exhibition of abject art at the MIT List Visual Arts Center, Jay maintains that abjection has been "paradoxically idealized" (237). This objection is unsurprising, given that it maintains the definitive view that art necessarily sublimates its content, and thus cannot help but beautify its objects. Abjection presents a special problem in this connection, however, since its subject matter is supposed to remain "repulsive." For Jay, abjection represented as art is abjection idealized, and to this extent it becomes a sham distortion of the foul material it wants to represent. His initial question, about why things like blood, pus, and disease, which have traditionally been rejected as a source of cultural value, are now being held up as optimal forms, is not unrelated to his concern about political activism, since idealized objects hold themselves aloof from the nitty-gritty mess of what it means to engage in social problems, and so entail political inertia. Because Kristeva posits an objectless condition that precedes entry into a symbolic order that depends on a subject/object split, Jay concludes that she wants a "state of perfect desublimation, which somehow frees itself entirely of some power of restriction and distinction, whether we call it symbolic language, patriarchal law or the formal organization of the body" (245).

It is undoubtedly the case that making art of abject objects deabjectifies them, but so what? Sublimation is, in effect, an instance of our unremitting dependency upon the symbolic, and the psychosis involved in abandoning this recourse. However, symbolic constructions can be more or less repressive, as Kristeva argues in *Revolution in Poetic Language*, where she wants to recover the mother tongue in and as poetry as a subversive strategy against rigid and phobic sublimations. To think of abjection in terms of lost subjects and inarticulate powers is to perpetuate myths of negation, the dream of abject content cast beyond the sphere of public language, beyond the "formal organization of the body"—into oblivion. While Kristeva's essay on abjection is not about desires toward perfect desublimation, it does register what is perhaps an inverse horror: that of "perfect sublimation," in which the unruly body is suppressed and denied by systems that revile their abjects. We might profitably refer to Kenneth Burke's codicil that man is the "symbol-making animal, rotten with perfection" (*Language as Symbolic Action* 16), by which he expresses a principle of sublimation: the idea that "compulsions to carry out the implications of one's terminology" can sometimes blind one to physical realities (19). Because the ordered symbolic and the integrated body are antipaths, both insisting on the proper and clean subject, the wasting body—uncivilized, unsanitary, offensive—is abandoned to silence, nonrecognition. The "powers of horror" are not, in Kristeva's theory, the fascistic oppressors and censors to which Jay vaguely alludes, but the terrors of the indomitable and dissipating body, and Kristeva's theory is not actually nostalgic. Granted, she features the abject body as a source of psychoanalytic insight and artistic inspiration (and perhaps thereby divulges a certain fascination with this body); however, the abject is nonetheless an object of revulsion, always a potential "horror." The disintegrating body/subject theorized by abjection has less to do with desire for a desublimated realm of being than it has to do with the perception that such a realm is beyond the bounds of human sense, perception, and possibility. *Powers of Horror* is not about desire to return to the void of the pre-Oedipal womb, but about how subjectivity is established through the very repudiation of the vacuity that it represents. Jay renounces this "ideal" vacuity, yet his own rejection of abject representation itself constructs an ideal: that of the unrepresentable other, defiant of our comprehensibility even as it is paradoxically conscripted as other. Kristeva recognizes both the necessary initiation of the subject into language and the tyranny of a symbolic order that denies the recalcitrant body of decay, death, and desire.

4. Susan Wendell has recently offered a striking appeal to feminism to acknowledge that the bodies we inhabit do not always enable us in the ways that we would like and are not always under our control. Afflicted with a fairly severe case of chronic fatigue-immune dysfunction syndrome (CFIDS), Wendell takes on the mind/body dualism, asserting that there may be physiological and psychological reasons for us to sometimes want to escape our bodies. Because physically impaired or challenged people are so heavily associated with their "disabled" bodies and not considered to have a self apart from those bodies, because people forget about that "person inside" the disabled body, detaching from that body may be advantageous or even necessary. When one becomes disabled, the need to define an inner self, in contradistinction to the suffering body, becomes a coping mechanism and a survival strategy.

5. Kyle Norwood notes that abjection occupies Frost, who "treats human evasions [of the horror of death] with an uneasy combination of protest and acceptance" (57). Norwood uses the concept of abjection to understand of "the unnamable 'something to be scared of' that haunts several of Frost's finest poems" (57), discussing the symbolic contract as a way to "know and control" (60). The "Home Burial" husband's way of "dealing with death and grief is to appeal to community standards and larger natural continuities, and thus to avoid taking loss too personally" (61), something the wife in the poem is unable to do, and so she keeps abjection "in imagination, within her house" (62). Norwood concludes, "If Frost's characters evade the abject, his poems do not; instead, they remain haunted by images of the unnamable, acknowledging that for the poet and for the reader, there is always 'something to be scared of'" (72).

6. Medical aesthetics has also become a busy paramedical industry that has expanded the activities of what had been known as cosmetology. For instance, the Hudson Valley School of Medical Aesthetics offers a course of study in

such subjects as hair removal, dermabrasion, and makeup techniques, preparing its students to pass the state licensing examination in aesthetics. Anna-Dee Rinehart identifies an "evolving field of medical aesthetics," understood as "the combined science of medicine and the art of aesthetics utilized to assess and manage facial conditions with a scientific approach including caring for the social, physical and psychological perspectives" (3).

7. Several studies on self/other distinctions, documented in Nancy Chodorow's *Feminism and Psychoanalytic Theory*, support the contention that men may be ill equipped to interiorize our abjection. Chodorow writes, "Women's biosexual experiences (menstruation, coitus, pregnancy, childbirth, lactation) all involve some challenge to the boundaries of her body ego ("me/"not-me" in relation to her blood or milk, to a man who penetrates her, to a child once part of her body)" (59). While Chodorow features this evidence in a negative light for women, arguing that such experiences of "boundary confusion" enlarge women's "guilt and self-blame for the other's unhappiness; shame and embarrassment at the other's actions" (58), I would stress "boundary confusion," alternatively, as facilitating compassionate solidarity with others, and hold it up as an ethical and philosophic model for men as well as women.

Works Cited

Adams, Jan R. *Everything Women of Color Should Know About Cosmetic Surgery.* New York: St. Martin's, 2000.

"Ad of Reeve Walking Gets Cheers, Cautions." *Palm Beach Post* Feb. 1, 2000: 10A.

"Age Defying Women." *The Oprah Winfrey Show.* WPTV, West Palm Beach. May 5, 2000.

Agonito, Rosemary, ed. *History of Ideas on Woman.* New York: Perigree, 1977.

Alliez, Eric, and Michel Feher. "Reflections of a Soul." Trans. Janet Lloyd. *Fragments for a History of the Body.* Part 2. Ed. Michel Feher et al. New York: Zone, 1989. 46–85.

Althusser, Louis. *Lenin and Philosophy and Other Essays.* Trans. Ben Brewster. New York: Monthly Review, 1971.

American Society for Aesthetic Plastic Surgery. "2001 Statistics." <http://www.surgery.org/statistics/html>. Oct. 20, 2002.

"Anna's Aloha Body." *A Personal Story.* The Learning Channel. Adelphia Cable Television Channel 49, Boca Raton, FL. June 7, 2002.

Bakan, David. *Disease, Pain, and Sacrifice: Toward a Psychology of Suffering.* Chicago: U of Chicago P, 1968.

Balsamo, Anne. *Technologies of the Gendered Body: Reading Cyborg Women.* Durham: Duke UP, 1996.

"Barbie Loses Butterfly Tattoo." *Palm Beach Post* June 9, 1999: 2A.

"Barbie's High-Kicking Legs Debut as Prosthetic Fingers." *Palm Beach Post* August 27, 2000: 2A.

Barnes, Julian E., and Greg Winter. "Stressed Out? Bad Knee? Relief Promised in a Juice." *New York Times* May 27, 2001: 1, 14.

Bataille, Georges. *Erotism: Death & Sensuality.* Trans. Mary Dalwood. San Francisco: City Lights, 1986.

Baudrillard, Jean. "Plastic Surgery for the Other." Trans. Francois Debrix. *CTHEORY.* Eds. Arthur Kroker and Marilouise Kroker. Nov. 22, 1995. <http://ctheory.com>.

"Beauty Is Only Skin Deep." Advertisement. *Palm Beach County Notables.* Special advertising supplement to *Palm Beach Post* Jan. 1, 1999: 16.

Beauvoir, Simone de. *The Second Sex.* Trans. E. M. Parshley. New York: Vintage, 1973.

Bersani, Leo. *The Freudian Body.* New York: Columbia UP, 1986.

Bordo, Susan. *The Male Body: A New Look at Men in Public and in Private.* New York: Farrar, Straus, and Giroux, 1999.

———. *Unbearable Weight: Feminism, Western Culture, and the Body.* Berkeley: U of California P, 1993.

———. *Twilight Zones: The Hidden Life of Cultural Images from Plato to O.J.* Berkeley: U of California P, 1997.

Brand, Peggy Zeglin, and Carolyn Korsmeyer, eds. *Feminism and Tradition in Aesthetics.* University Park: Pennsylvania SUP, 1995.

Breathnach, Sarah Ban. "Mirror Image." *O, The Oprah Magazine.* Oct. 2000. 202. Excerpted from *The Simple Abundance Companion.* New York: Warner Books, 2000. 78–79.

Brennan, Teresa. *The Interpretation of the Flesh: Freud and Femininity.* New York: Routledge, 1992.

Brown, Peter. *The Body and Society: Men, Women, and Sexual Renunciation in Early Christianity.* New York: Columbia UP, 1988.

Burgess, Patricia. *Cosmetic Surgery Without Fear: How to Make Safe Choices and Informed Decisions.* Atlanta: Cosmetic Surgery Consultants, 2000.

Burke, Edmund. *A Philosophical Enquiry into the Origin of Our Ideas of the Sublime and the Beautiful.* Ed. James T. Boulton. London: Routledge, 1958.

Burke, Kenneth. *A Rhetoric of Motives.* 1950. Berkeley: U of California P, 1969.

Bynum, Caroline Walker. *Fragmentation and Redemption: Essays on Gender and the Human Body in Medieval Religion.* New York: Zone, 1991.

Camille, Michael. The Gothic Idol: Ideology and Image-Making in Medieval Art. Cambridge, Eng.: Cambridge UP, 1991.

Caputi, Jane. *The Age of Sex Crime.* Bowling Green, OH: Popular Press, 1987.

Cash, Thomas F., and Thomas Pruzinsky, eds. *Body Images: Development, Deviance, and Change.* New York: Guilford, 1990.

Cassell, Eric J. *The Nature of Suffering and the Goals of Medicine.* New York: Oxford UP, 1991.

Chodorow, Nancy J. *Feminism and Psychoanalytic Theory.* New Haven: Yale UP, 1989. "Choose Your Life." *The Oprah Winfrey Show.* WPTV, West Palm Beach. June 21, 2000.

"Classically Contoured." Advertisement. *Palm Beach County Notables.* Special advertising supplement to *Palm Beach Post* Mar. 21, 2001. 4.

"Clinical Studies Show that Aging is Now a Treatable Disease." Radio Advertisement. WIOD AM. June 26, 2000.

"Cosmetic Surgery." *Talk of the Nation. Host: Ray Suarez.* NPR online. March 24, 1998. <http://www.npr.org>.

Covino, Deborah Caslav. "Abject Criticism." *Genders* (Fall 2000). <http://genders.org/g32/g32_covino.html>.

Creed, Barbara. *The Monstrous-Feminine: Film, Feminism, Psychoanalysis.* New York: Routledge, 1993.

"Dad's Nose Goes." *A Personal Story.* The Learning Channel. Adelphia Cable Television Channel 49, Boca Raton, FL. 10 June 2002.

Dante Alighieri. *The Divine Comedy.* Trans. John D. Sinclair. New York: Oxford UP, 1939.

Davis, Kathy. "My Body is My Art: Cosmetic Surgery as Feminist Utopia?" *Embodied Practices: Feminist Perspectives on the Body.* Ed. Kathy Davis. London: Sage, 1997. 168–81.

———. *Reshaping the Female Body: The Dilemma of Cosmetic Surgery.* New York: Routledge, 1995.

Diamond, Irene, and Lee Quinby, ed. *Feminism and Foucault: Reflections on Resistance.* Boston: Northeastern UP, 1988.

Dinnerstein, Dorothy. *The Mermaid and the Minotaur.* New York : Harper, 1977.

"Does This Make Me Look Fat?" *The Oprah Winfrey Show.* WPTV, West Palm Beach. February 23, 2001.

Douglas, Mary. *Purity and Danger: An Analysis of the Concepts of Pollution and Taboo.* Boston: Routledge & Kegan Paul, 1966.

DuCille, Ann. "Black Barbie and the Deep Play of Difference." *Skin Trade.* Cambridge: Harvard UP, 1996. Extract rpt. *Feminism and Cultural Studies.* Ed. Morag Schiach. New York: Oxford UP, 1999. 106–32.

Edwards, Jonathan. *The Saints, When Absent From the Body, Are Present With The Lord.* Ed. John Mark Ockerbloom. Online Books at the University of Pennsylvania. 1999. May 21, 2001. <http://www.ccel.org/e/edwards/absent_body/absent_body1.0.pdf>.

El Saadawi, Nawal. "Women, Dissidence, and Creativity." Lecture. Florida Atlantic University. October 19, 1999.

Engler, Alan. BodySculpture: Plastic Surgery of the Body For Men & Women. New York: Hudson, 1988.

Faludi, Susan. Backlash: The Undeclared War Against American Women. New York: Crown, 1991.

———. Stiffed: The Betrayal of the American Man. New York: William Morrow, 1999.

"Fatima's Flawless Nose." A Personal Story. The Learning Channel. Adelphia Cable Television Channel 49, Boca Raton, FL. June 10, 2002.

Feher, Michel, ed. Fragments for a History of the Body. 3 Vols. New York: Zone, 1989.

Fiedler, Leslie. Tyranny of the Normal: Essays on Bioethics, Theology & Myth. Boston: D. R. Godine, 1996.

Forehead Lift. Pamphlet. Arlington Heights, IL: American Society of Plastic and Reconstructive Surgeons, 1997.

Foucault, Michel. The History of Sexuality 1 : An Introduction. Trans. Robert Hurley. New York : Pantheon, 1978.

———. The History of Sexuality 3: The Care of the Self. Trans. Robert Hurley. New York: Random House, 1980.

Friday, Nancy. The Power of Beauty. New York: HarperCollins, 1996.

Frost, Robert. "Provide, Provide." The Poetry of Robert Frost. New York: Holt, Rinehart and Winston, 1969. 307.

Gail, Susan. Cosmetic Surgery: Before, Between and After. La Jolla: Mélange Unlimited, 2000.

Gaines, Jane. "White Privilege and Looking Relations: Race and Gender in Feminist Film Theory." Feminism & Film. Ed. E. Ann Kaplan. New York: Oxford UP, 2000. 336–55.

Gallagher, Catherine, and Thomas Laqueur, eds. The Making of the Modern Body: Sexuality and Society in the Nineteenth Century. Berkeley: U of California P, 1987.

Gallop, Jane. Thinking Through the Body. New York: Columbia, 1988.

Ganny, Charlee, and Susan J. Collini. Two Girlfriends Get Real About Cosmetic Surgery: A Woman-to-Woman Guide to Today's Most Popular Cosmetic Procedures. Los Angeles: Renaissance, 2000.

"Gary Zukav on Fear." The Oprah Winfrey Show. WPTV, West Palm Beach. June 5, 2000.

"Gary Zukav on Finding Meaning & Purpose in Your Life." *The Oprah Winfrey Show.* WPTV, West Palm Beach. Feb. 10, 2000.

"Gary Zukav on How to Get Your Power Back." *The Oprah Winfrey Show.* WPTV, West Palm Beach. Jan. 4, 2001.

Gaynor, Alan. *Everything You Always Wanted to Know About Cosmetic Surgery But Couldn't Afford to Ask.* New York: Broadway, 1998.

Gelfant, Benjamin. *Cosmetic Surgery: A Patient's Guide.* Vancouver: Flapartz, 1997.

Gilman, Sander. *Creating Beauty to Cure the Soul: Race and Psychology in the Shaping of Aesthetic Surgery.* Durham: Duke UP, 1998.

———. *Disease and Representation: Images of Illness from Madness to AIDS.* Ithaca: Cornell UP, 1988.

———. *Making the Body Beautiful: A Cultural History of Aesthetic Surgery.* Princeton: Princeton UP, 1999.

Gonzalez-Ulloa, Mario, ed. *The Creation of Aesthetic Plastic Surgery.* New York: Springer-Verlag, 1985.

Good, Byron J. "A Body in Pain: The Making of a World of Chronic Pain." *Pain as Human Experience: An Anthropological Perspective.* Eds. Mary-Jo DelVecchio Good et al. Berkeley: U of California P, 1992. 29–48.

Grant, Priscilla. "Face Time." *Modern Maturity* March/April 2001: 56–63.

Grosz, Elizabeth. *Sexual Subversions: Three French Feminists.* Boston: Allen and Unwin, 1989.

Haiken, Elizabeth. *Venus Envy: A History of Cosmetic Surgery.* Baltimore: Johns Hopkins UP, 1997.

Hall, Stuart. "On Postmodernism and Articulation: An Interview with Stuart Hall." Ed. Lawrence Grossberg. *Journal of Communication Inquiry* 10.2 (1986): 45–60.

Haraway, Donna. Modest_Witness@Second_Millennium*: FemaleMan_ Meets_OncoMouse.* New York: Routledge, 1997.

———. "The Promises of Monsters." *Cultural Studies.* Ed. Lawrence Grossberg et al. New York: Routledge, 1992. 295–337. Routledge, 1997.

Heartney, Eleanor. "Foreword: Cutting Two Ways with Beauty." *Beauty Matters.* Ed. Peggy Zeglin Brand. Bloomington: Indiana UP, 2000. xiii–xv.

Hein, Hilde, and Carolyn Korsmeyer, eds. *Aesthetics in Feminist Perspective.* Bloomington: Indiana UP, 1993.

Henry, Kimberly A., and Penny S. Heckaman. *Plastic Surgery Sourcebook.* Los Angeles: Lowell, 1997.

Hiassen, Carl. *Sick Puppy: A Novel.* New York: Alfred A. Knopf, 1999.

"High Tech Communications Makeovers." *The Oprah Winfrey Show*. WPTV, West Palm Beach. January 31, 2000.

Hinderer, Ulrich. "Early History of the ISAPS." 1995. International Society for Aesthetic Plastic Surgery. July 19, 2000. <http://www.worldplastic-surgery.org/pdf/historyisaps.pdf>.

"The History of Plastic Surgery." 2000. American Society of Plastic Surgeons. May 7, http://www.plasticsurgery.org/overview/pshistry.htm.

Horgan, John. "Beyond Viagra." *The New York Times Book Review*. Supplement to the *New York Times*. August 15, 1999.

Houser, Craig, et al. *Abject Art: Repulsion and Desire in American Art*. New York: Whitney Museum, 1993.

"How Would It Be to Have the Wisdom of the Years and the Face of Youth?" Advertisement. *Palm Beach County Notables*. Special advertising supplement to *Palm Beach Post*. Sept. 29, 1999: 4.

Hurst, Fannie. *Imitation of Life*. New York: Harper & Row, 1990.

Irigaray, Luce. *Speculum of the Other Woman*. Trans. Gillian Gill. Ithaca: Cornell UP, 1985.

Jameson, Frederic. *The Political Unconscious: Narrative as a Socially Symbolic Act*. Ithaca: Cornell University Press, 1981.

Johnson, Mark. *The Body in the Mind: The Bodily Basis of Meaning, Imagination, and Reason*. Chicago: U of Chicago P, 1987.

Joyce, James. *Ulysses*. New York : Vintage, 1986.

Kamps, Louisa. "Mothers Who Think: Labia Envy." *Salon.com*. Mar. 16, 1998. <http://www.salon.com/mwt/feature/1998/03/16feature.html>.

Kant, Immanuel. *Observations on the Feeling of the Beautiful and Sublime*. Trans. John T. Goldthwait. Berkeley: U of California P, 1965.

Kaw, Eugenia. "Medicalization of Racial Features: Asian-American Women and Cosmetic Surgery." *The Politics of Women's Bodies: Sexuality, Appearance, and Behavior*. Ed. Rose Weitz. New York: Oxford UP, 1998. 167–83.

Kirwan, James. *Beauty*. Manchester: Manchester UP, 1999.

Kristeva, Julia. *Desire in Language: A Semiotic Approach to Literature and Art*. Ed. Leon S. Roudiez. Trans. Thomas Gora, Alice Jardine, and Leon S. Roudiez. New York: Columbia UP, 1980.

———. *Powers of Horror: An Essay on Abjection*. Trans. Leon S. Roudiez. New York: Columbia UP, 1982.

———. *Revolution in Poetic Language*. Trans. Margaret Waller. New York: Columbia UP, 1984.

———. "Stabat Mater." *Tales of Love*. Trans. Leon S. Roudiez. New York: Columbia UP, 1987. 234–63.

———. "The System and the Speaking Subject." *Times Literary Supplement* October 12, 1973. Rpt. *The Kristeva Reader.* Ed. Toril Moi. New York: Columbia UP, 1986. 24–33.

Kroker, Arthur, and Michael Weinstein. *Data Trash: The Theory of the Virtual Class.* New York: St. Martin's, 1994.

Kuhn, Andrea. "'What's the matter, Trevor? Scared of something?'" Representing the Monstrous-feminine in *Candyman.*" Erfurt Electronic Studies in English. 2000. <http://webdoc.gwdg.de/edoc/ia/eese/>.

Lacan, Jacques. "The Mirror Stage as Formative of the Function of the I as Revealed in Psychoanalytic Experience." *Ecrits.* Trans. Alan Sheridan. New York: Norton, 1977. 1–7.

Laqueur, Thomas. *Making Sex.* Cambridge: Harvard UP, 1990.

Leland, Dorothy J. "Subversion of Women's Agency in Psychoanalytic Feminism." *Revaluing French Feminism: Critical Essays on Difference, Agency, and Culture.* Ed. Nancy Fraser and Sandra Lee Bartky. 113–35.

"Lifestyle Makeovers." *The Oprah Winfrey Show.* WPTV, West Palm Beach. May 29, 2000.

"Light in Jodi's Eyes." *A Personal Story.* The Learning Channel. Adelphia Cable Television Channel 49, Boca Raton, FL. June 17, 2002.

Linton, Simi. *Claiming Disability: Knowledge and Identity.* New York: New York UP, 1998.

Little, Margaret Olivia. "Cosmetic Surgery, Suspect Norms, and the Ethics of Complicity." *Enhancing Human Traits: Ethical and Social Implications.* Ed. Erik Parens. Washington, D.C.: Georgetown UP, 1998. 162–76.

Loftus, Jean M. *The Smart Woman's Guide to Plastic Surgery.* Chicago: Contemporary, 2000.

Loraux, Nicole. "Therefore, Socrates Is Immortal." Trans. Janet Lloyd. *Fragments for a History of the Human Body.* Part 2. Ed. Michel Feher. New York: Zone, 12–45.

Luciano, Lynne. *Looking Good: Male Body Image in Modern America.* New York: Hill and Wang, 2001.

Lupton, Deborah. *Medicine as Culture: Illness, Disease, and the Body in Western Societies.* Thousand Oaks: Sage, 1994.

Marcuse, Herbert. *One Dimensional Man.* Boston: Beacon, 1964.

Marfuggi, Richard A. *Plastic Surgery: What You Need To Know Before, During, and After.* New York: Perigree, 1998.

Matousek, Mark. "Start the Conversation: The *Modern Maturity* Guide to End-of-Life Care." Special pull-out section. *Modern Maturity.* Sept.-Oct. 2000: 51–59.

Mauldin, Kendra. "Barbie at 40, No Escaping Gravity." *Palm Beach Post* March 6, 1999: 1D.

"Millennium Makeovers with Tyra Banks." *The Oprah Winfrey Show.* WPTV, West Palm Beach. Jan. 3, 2000.

Morgan, Kathryn Pauly. "Women and the Knife: Cosmetic Surgery and the Colonization of Women's Bodies." *Hypatia* 6.3: 25–53. Rpt. *The Politics of Women's Bodies: Sexuality, Appearance, and Behavior.* Ed. Rose Weitz. New York: Oxford UP, 1998. 147–66.

Morris, David B. *The Culture of Pain.* Berkeley: U of California P, 1991.

———. "How to Live Forever." *Illness and Culture in the Postmodern Age.* Berkeley: U of California P, 1998: 1–20.

Morrison, Toni. *The Bluest Eye.* New York: Penguin, 1994.

Mr. Sardonicus. Dir. William Castle. Perf. Guy Rolfe, Oscar Homolka, Tina Woodward. Columbia, 1961.

Mulvey, Laura. "Visual Pleasure and Narrative Cinema." *Screen* 16.3 (1976): 6–18.

Norwood, Kyle. "The Work of Not Knowing: Robert Frost and the Abject." *Southwest Review* 78.1 (Win. 1993): 57–72.

"Now they call them botox 'seminars'—in Las Vegas." Oct. 20, 2002. <http://www.bayarea.com/mld/mercurynews/living>

Nuland, Sherwin B. *How We Die: Reflections on Life's Final Chapter.* New York: Vintage, 1993.

———. "A Munch Moment: 'The Scream' or 'The Whimper.'" *The New York Times.* February 27, 2000: WK5.

Null, Gary. *Gary Null's Ultimate Anti-Aging Program.* New York: Kensington, 1999.

O'Donnell, Patrick, and Robert Con Davis, eds. *Intertextuality and Contemporary American Fiction.* Baltimore : Johns Hopkins UP, 1989.

"Oh What a Piece of Work Is Man." *Chicago Hope.* CBS. WPEC, West Palm Beach, FL. October 7, 1999.

Oliver, Kelly. *Reading Kristeva: Unraveling the Double-bind.* Bloomington: Indiana UP, 1993.

Oliver, Michael. *Understanding Disability: From Theory to Practice.* New York: St. Martin's, 1996.

"Oprah's Book Club." *The Oprah Winfrey Show.* WPTV, West Palm Beach. May 26, 2000.

"Oprah Talks with Elie Wiesel." *O, The Oprah Magazine* Nov. 2000: 232–37, 284–86.

Pacteau, Francette. *The Symptom of Beauty.* Cambridge: Harvard UP, 1994.

Parens, Erik, ed. *Enhancing Human Traits: Ethical and Social Implications.* Washington D.C.: Georgetown UP, 1998.

Pickel, Mary Lou, and Sonja Isger. "Barbie Exhibit Dresses Up Teachers' Career Points." *Palm Beach Post.* May 22, 1999: 1D, 5D.

"A Place for Thanks Giving." *O, The Oprah Magazine* Nov. 2000: 120–22.

"Plastic Surgery." *Talk of the Nation.* National Public Radio. Mar. 24, 1998.

"Plastic Surgery Indications." Pamphlet. Arlington Heights, IL: American Society of Plastic and Reconstructive Surgeons, 1997.

"Plastic Surgery Today." Advertising supplement to *USA Today.* Oct. 13, 2000.

"Pride Scooters." Advertisement. *Modern Maturity.* Sept.-Oct. 2000: 105.

Pruzinsky, Thomas, and Milton T. Edgerton. "Body-Image Change in Cosmetic Plastic Surgery." *Body Images: Development, Deviance, and Change.* Ed. Thomas F. Cash and Thomas Pruzinsky. New York: Guilford, 1990. 217–36.

Ratcliffe, Krista. *Anglo-American Feminist Challenges to the Rhetorical Traditions: Virginia Woolf, Mary Daly, Adrienne Rich.* Carbondale: Southern Illinois UP, 1996.

Rathbun, Ron. "Words To Grow On." Excerpted from *The Way Is Within: A Spiritual Journey. O, The Oprah Magazine* Sept. 2000: 140–42.

"Rediscover the Beauty in Your Eyes." Advertisement. *Palm Beach County Notables.* Special advertising supplement to *Palm Beach Post* July 19, 2000: 4.

Reineke, Martha. "'This Is My Body': Reflections on Abjection, Anorexia, and Medieval Women Mystics." *Journal of the American Academy of Religion* 58.2 (1990): 245–65.

Rey, Roselyne. *The History of Pain.* Translated by Louise Elliott Wallace et al. Cambridge: Harvard UP, 1995.

Riddell, Jennifer L. "The Abject Object: A Recent History of the Ephemeral Found Object in Contemporary Art." *New Art Examiner* 23 (Oct. 1995): 26–53.

Rinehart, Anna-Dee. "Medical Aesthetics: Developing Working Relationships Between Physicians and Aestheticians." May 19, 2001 <http://www.medicalaesthetics.com/aestheticianphysician.htm>.

Rorty, Richard. "Tale of Two Disciplines." *Beauty and the Critic: Aesthetics in an Age of Cultural Studies.* Ed. James Soderholm. Tuscaloosa: Alabama UP, 1997. 208–24.

Russo, Mary. *The Female Grotesque: Risk, Excess, and Modernity.* New York: Routledge, 1995.

Sabbath, Dan, and Mandel Hall. *End Product: The First Taboo.* New York: Urizen, 1977.

Sapolsky, Harvey M. "The Truly Endless Frontier." *Technology Review* (Nov./Dec. 1995): 37–42.

Sarnoff, Deborah S., and Joan Swirsky. *Beauty and the Beam: Your Complete Guide to Cosmetic Laser Surgery.* New York: St. Martin's Griffin, 1998.

Scarry, Elaine. *The Body in Pain: The Making and Unmaking of the World.* New York: Oxford UP, 1985.

———. *On Beauty and Being Just.* Princeton: Princeton UP, 1999.

Sedgwick, Eve. "Gender Criticism." *Redrawing the Boundaries: The Transformation of English and American Literary Studies.* Eds. Stephen Greenblatt and Giles Gunn. New York: MLA, 1992. 271–302.

"Sela Ward on Ageism in Hollywood." *The Oprah Winfrey Show.* WPTV, West Palm Beach. Feb. 28, 2000.

Shah, Diane K. "Lucky Star." *Modern Maturity.* May-June 2000: 30–35.

Shelley, Mary. *Frankenstein, or The Modern Prometheus.* New York: Penguin, 1992.

Siegel, Rudolph E. *Galen On Sense Perception: His doctrines, Observations and Experiments on Vision, Hearing, Smell, Taste, Touch and Pain, and Their Historical Sources.* New York: Karger, 1970.

Silvers, Anita. "A Fatal Attraction to Normalizing: Treating Disabilities as Deviations from 'Species-Typical' Functioning." *Enhancing Human Traits: Ethical and Social Implications.* Ed. Erik Parens. Washington D.C.: Georgetown UP, 1998. 95–123.

Smaller, Margaret. "Intertextuality: An Interview with Kristeva." *Intertextuality and Contemporary American Fiction.* Eds. Patrick O'Donnell and Robert Con Davis. Johns Hopkins UP, 1989.

Soderholm, James. "Introduction." *Beauty and the Critic: Aesthetics in an Age of Cultural Studies.* Ed. James Soderholm. Tuscaloosa: Alabama UP, 1997. 1–12.

Sontag, Susan. *Illness as Metaphor* and *Aids and its Metaphors.* New York: Anchor, 1990.

Spear, Scott L., ed. *Surgery of the Breast: Principles and Art.* Philadelphia: Lippincott-Raven, 1998.

Spelman, Elizabeth V. *Fruits of Sorrow: Framing Our Attention to Suffering.* Boston: Beacon P, 1997.

Squire, Corinne. "Empowering Women? *The Oprah Winfrey Show.*" *Media Studies: A Reader, 2000.* Ed. Paul Marris and Sue Thornham. New York: New York UP, 2000. 354-67.

Stafford, Barbara. *Body Criticism: Imaging the Unseen in Enlightenment Art and Medicine.* Cambridge: MIT, 1991.

Suleiman, Susan, ed. *The Female Body in Western Culture: Contemporary Perspectives.* Cambridge: Harvard UP, 1986.

Sullivan, Deborah A. *Cosmetic Surgery: The Cutting Edge of Commercial Medicine in America.* New Brunswick: Rutgers UP, 2001.

"Take It Off!" *The Oprah Winfrey Show.* WPTV, West Palm Beach. Feb. 1, 2000.

Tazi, Nadia. "Celestial Bodies: A Few Stops on the Way to Heaven." Trans. Anna Cancogni. *Fragments for a History of the Body.* Part 2. Ed. Michel Feher et al. New York: Zone, 1989. 518–52.

Thomson, Rosemary Garland. *Extraordinary Bodies: Figuring Physical Disability in American Culture and Literature.* New York: Columbia UP, 1997.

Toughill, Kelly. "Retouching Nature's Way: Is Cosmetic Surgery Worth It?" *Toronto Star.* Feb. 1, 1990: A17.

Tucker, Peter. "Skin of Desire, Skin of Terror: A Comparison." *The Animist.* Jan. 2000. <http://animist2000.netgazer.net.au/pg000032.html>.

Twardowski, Lynda. "The Queen of Talk." *The Unofficial Oprah Winfrey Tribute.* Magazine. Bannockburn, IL: H & S Media 2000: 30–39.

"U. of Alberta Course Examines Mystique of Oprah Winfrey." *The Chronicle of Higher Education.* Oct. 6 2000: A12.

Vernant, Jean-Pierre. "Dim Body, Dazzling Body." Trans. Anne M. Wilson. *Fragments for a History of the Body.* Part 1. Ed. Michel Feher, et al. New York: Zone, 1989. 18–47.

"Weight Loss First." *The Oprah Winfrey Show.* WPTV, West Palm Beach. Feb. 2, 2000.

Weiss, Gail A. *Body Images: Embodiment as Intercorporeality.* New York: Routledge, 1999.

Wheeler, David L. "Could Boys Get 'Barbie Syndrome'?" *The Chronicle of Higher Education* June 11, 1999: A22.

"When Choosing A Plastic Surgeon, An Artistic Touch Means As Much As Great Credentials." *The Real Yellow Pages: Boca Raton and Deerfield Beach.* Boca Raton, FL: Bell South Advertising and Publishing, 2000: 1014.

Willis, Susan. "I Shop Therefore I Am: Is There A Place for Afro-American Culture in Commodity Culture?" *Changing Our Own Words: Essays on Criticism, Theory, and Writing by Black Women.* Ed. Cheryl A. Wall. New Brunswick: Rutgers UP, 1989. Rpt. *Feminisms: An Anthology of Literary Theory and Criticism.* Eds. Robyn R. Warhol and Diane Price Herndl. New Brunswick: Rutgers UP, 1997. 992–1008.

Wilson, Andrew. "The Art Experience." *Art Monthly* 190 (Oct. 1995): 3–6.

Wolf, Naomi. *The Beauty Myth: How Images of Beauty Are Used Against Women.* New York: W. Morrow, 1991.

"Words You Can Trust." *O, The Oprah Magazine* Oct. 2000: 140–142.

Wyer, E. Bingo. *The Unofficial Guide to Cosmetic Surgery.* New York: Macmillan, 1999.

Yaeger, Patricia. "The 'Language of Blood': Toward a Maternal Sublime." *Genre* 25 (Spring 1992): 5–24.

Zeyl, Donald, trans. *Timaeus. Plato, Complete Works.* Ed. John M. Cooper. Indianapolis: Hackett, 1997: 1224–91.

Index